Cumbrian Dialect

By the same author

CHESHIRE CHATTER
CUMBRIAN CHAT
DERBYSHIRE DRAWL
LANCASHIRE DIALECT
LANKY TWANG
NOTTS NATTER
YORKSHIRE YAMMER

Cumbrian Dialect

by

Peter Wright

Dalesman Books
1979

The Dalesman Publishing Company Limited,
Clapham (via Lancaster), North Yorkshire

First published 1979

ISBN: 0 85206 563 9

Printed in Great Britain by Galava Printing Company Limited,
Hallam Road, Nelson, Lancashire.

Contents

INTRODUCTION

CUMBRIAN dialect has never quite received the attention it deserves, and so this book tries to remedy this deficiency. It parallels two other Dalesman publications, J. Waddington-Feather's *Yorkshire Dialect* and my *Lancashire Dialect*. It is also a more serious sequel to my *Cumbrian Chat,* the latest in a series of Dalesman mini-books which are fairly light-hearted efforts to introduce county dialects (Others include *The Lanky Twang, The Yorkshire Yammer* and *The Derbyshire Drawl.*) I would not want, however, to belittle these popular books because great efforts have been made to cram them with useful information, and only in such ways is it possible to obtain the mass feedback necessary to provide a more serious work of this kind. But if you wish shortly to study the dialects of other counties, you may wish among other things to look at them.

My first introduction to Cumbrian dialect was around Whitsun, 1950, when as first fieldworker for the Leeds University *Survey of English Dialects* I was sent out for three weeks to *Kirkby Stevvan* (Kirkby Stephen), Ambleside and Keswick to make preliminary recordings by asking in each place the 1800 odd questions of the drafted Dieth-Orton questionnaire, whilst paying close attention to anything else being said spontaneously. Unfortunately the answers were used only to see how well the questions worked (a very necessary precaution) and the results themselves were not analysed, chiefly it seems because they were not taken from small rural communities as nearly all the other results of the Leeds survey were. Far worse, though not surprisingly after this great lapse of time, the records have apparently been lost.

What I recall most vividly from that intensive holiday are the very helpful people met, like the great dialect speaker at Kirkby Stephen who insisted on telling my fortune, and at Keswick the veterans at the bowling green, along with a marvellous nature expert and another whose speciality was the islands of Derwentwater. There was also, for example, William M. Vity of Ambleside, who talked to me in a roomful of clocks and who died aged 87 in June 1968. He had much knowledge of the district and many people wanted him to write it down, though he never did.

Losing the recordings has, however, brought advantages in spurring me to update the information by repeated surveys round Cumbria, including another two quite recently. The object, despite concentrating on the speech of the old timers, is to show the dialect of today, not of a far-away past. One technical matter to explain is the inclusion of variant spellings, like *hoo* and *oo* (how), or *aboot* and *about*. This is deliberate, to accord with the localities mentioned within this large county and with the fluctuations in any individual's speech. By such methods the steady aim has been to present in the following pages a realistic picture of the modern dialect.

ACKNOWLEDGEMENTS

PRIDE of place must go to all the kindly informants without whom this book would have been impossible. They include: W.G. Bunting of Kendal; Keith Coates of Rydal; Eric Dobson of Troutbeck; J. Elliot of Carlisle; Harold Forsyth of Kirkbampton; Tom Foster, J.P., of Millom; J.R. Hardisty of Grasmere; J.W. Hogarth of Kendal; Harry Kellett and family of Dalton; Bill Mallinson, now of Barrow; H.W. Robinson of Gatebeck; Mr and Mrs E. Walker of Windermere and employees of Vickers at Barrow and United Steel at Workington.

Other informants would be surprised to see their remarks and words here because they were collected 'on the wing' from natural conversation in all sorts of unlikely spots, with no pen or paper visible. Great help came too from other directions, notably: The Lakeland Dialect Society through its indefatigable editor Ted Relph, who kindly gave permission to reprint material from my articles in their Journals nos. 29, 30 and 39, where further informants are named; the staff of Barrow, Carlisle and Lancaster public libraries; Professor G.L. Brook, formerly of Manchester University; Norman Nicholson, well-known writer of Millom; and Dr. Rollinson of the Extramural Department of Liverpool University. To all I am most grateful.

1. Historical

MODERN Cumbria was formed in 1974 by amalgamating Cumberland, Westmorland and Lancashire North of the Sands, and so in considering the origins of Cumbrian dialect it is important to establish when these three counties were formed. Lancashire was apparently created about 1267, when the king put Roger de Lancaster in charge of it[1]. The early history of the two Lakeland counties is less easily extracted, for, although the terms *England* and *Scotland* now have precise enough meanings which have changed little for at least 800 years, the date at which the Tweed-Solway line became a political and ethnic boundary is unclear, although it was probably about 1032.

However, P.A. Wilson in a most carefully researched article[2] states that *Cymry* is from the earlier Celtic *Cambroges* signifying 'fellow-countrymen'. The *Anglo-Saxon Chronicle* has no entry containing the place name *Cumberland* earlier than 945, but evidence exists that there was once a text with some such form in King Alfred's reign. According to the *Chronicle* of Aethelweard[3], which was based on an original of the time of King Alfred, in 875 Halfdene the Dane left Repton with part of the Danish army to make war upon the Picts and the *Cumbri.* This, along with evidence of the placename *Cumbrae,* strongly suggests that in the later part of the ninth century a people calling themselves Cumbrians inhabited a wide area between what was then Northumbria and the Firth of Clyde. The church of Glasgow was equated with the bishopric of this Cumbrian kingdom.

The name *Westmorland* was in popular use for about two centuries, before, in about 1177, it became the name of the newly created county covering an area much larger than tenth century *Westmoringalond.* Eventually, to all except a handful of clerics in Glasgow, *Cumberland* had come to mean 'land south of the Solway'.

1. See **The Victoria County History.**
2. Cumberland & Westmorland Antiquarian Soc. **Transactions,** new series, vol. LXVI (1966), pp. 57-92.
3. Ed. A. Campbell, 1962, p.41.

Westmorland and *Copeland* were used in official documents in South Scotland in the reign of King David (1107-53) without any sense of ambiguity. P.A. Wilson concludes, 'Indeed, I have the impression that, had this region continued under Scottish rule, it would have been parcelled into three separate shires: Cumberland, that part of the modern county (i.e. before the planners produced Cumbria) belonging to the medieval diocese of Carlisle; Westmorland, that part of the medieval diocese belonging to the modern county of that name; and Copeland, that part of modern Cumberland which lies to the south and west of the medieval diocesan boundary.' How would present-day Cumbrian administrators like to cope with that?

WHERE IS THE DIALECT?

History has therefore made Cumbrian a group of related dialects, but with sharp divisions. Carlisle speech has tinges of County Durham's. The Eden valley speech is different and Wigton different again. The main watershed is an important factor, because the Eden valley may show Tyneside, North Riding and even West Riding influence, whereas the valleys dropping towards Morecambe Bay have Lancashire affinities. Yet the picture is even more complex. For example, even within the parish of *Gert Saffel* (Great Salkeld) the two straggling hamlets of North Dyke and South Dyke could be distinguished in speech by people who knew them.

Now, of course, ease of travel, mass education, radio and television have exerted their leavening influence, but the dialect is still quite vigorous. In Ambleside and Windermere it has to be searched for, more so in the latter. Good places for dialect are the more out-of-the way ones, up along the fell sides like Renwick or *Mellerby* (Melmerby) or up little valleys like Kentmere or out at the dale heads. Any farming community—and Cumbria is full of them—has plenty of dialect. But everywhere it depends partly on whom you meet.

WORD HISTORY

Etymology can teach us a good deal. As might be expected, Celtic influence is strong, much stronger than in most English counties. Celtic words include the following, with their Irish Gaelic origins in square brackets:
ask (newt) [*asc* (snake, adder)], *dunnock* (hedge-sparrow) [from its colour *donn* (dusty)], *hog* (year-old sheep) [*og* (young, a youth)], *mug* (ugly face) [*muig*], *noddy* (simpleton) [*naoidhe* (babe, infant)], *spunk* (spirit, vivacity) [*sponc* (touchwood, tinder)], *teg* (yearling

sheep) [*othaisg*].

Of Welsh descent appear to be *hub* (nave of wheel) [cf. Welsh *hwff* (lump)] and *shoddy* (waste in worsted mills) [cf. Welsh *sothach* (refuse)]. Here belongs also the 'rough-sounding' word in 'Shove that in yer gob (Consider that)', 'Shut yer gob! (Be quiet!), from Welsh *gob* (heap, mass).

The Manx variety of Gaelic has links with various Cumbrian words, which is really not surprising considering its proximity. Many a visitor climbing a little, say, near Boot in Eskdale has been astonished to see the Isle of Man so near. Cumbrian examples follow. Where they differ from their Manx equivalents, the latter have been shown in square brackets: *bleb* (blister, bubble), *bluett* (long-nosed skate), *broc* (badger), *broo* (hill-slope) [*broogh*], *buckie* (large whelk) [*buckee*], *chimla* (chimney) [*chimlee*].

The other outstanding foreign influence on Cumbrian terms is Scandinavian. It has been proved by Cumbrians working or on holiday in Iceland that their dialect words are understood there. *Laik* (to play) is readily understood by Icelanders, as is *dunk*. Cumbrians *dunk* their gingersnap,—compare Swedish dialect *dank* (moist field). Add to these *ley* for a scythe; *brant* (steep) as in Brantwood, Ruskin's home by Coniston Water; and *ootgang* for a public right of way from valley to fell. If someone grumbles, Ah've hurt mi lisk (groin) laikin' (playing) on a slape (slippery) steean i't' beck (stream), he has used four Scandinavian words, those translated in brackets.

On the farm you meet Scandinavian words in profusion. Ewes can be *souted* (diseased), sheep can be *kessen* (on their backs and unable to rise), and various animals *kenspecked* (branded, marked). There you have three adjectives from Old Norse. A cart-horse may be *kyavellin' aboot* (scratching about and digging in its feet as it tries to go down a steep hill), or a sheep may be seen acting similarly, *kyavellin' on a trod* (sheep-track). *Steg* for the gander is a dialect word once met over a much wider area, for example in Cheshire, but still heard in Lakeland. *Lowp* is another word of Viking ancestry, whilst yet another is *seave* (the rush) [Old Norse *sef*], preserved for example in Grasmere's *Seavy Close*. Additional ones are: *addle* (earn), *garth* (yard) in *sta(ck)garth* (stackyard), *keck* (to tip), *ket* (rubbish), *lowse* (finish) for example in, 'It's lowsin'-time', *mawk* (maggot), *neef* (fist), *recklin* (smallest pig of litter); and probably *stee* (ladder) and *teem* (pour). No language enthusiast listening to Cumbrian can doubt that Norsemen like the Celts have in past ages been firmly established in these parts.

The French element is much smaller. One horrible example is *sturdy*, a disease whereby a bladder of grubs forms on the side of a sheep's brain so that it spins and staggers. It is a shortening of French *etourdi* (giddy). This reminds us that all sorts of other abbreviations enter the dialect—everything from *po*, a childish shortening of *chamberpot,* to remarks like 'T'match 'll be on t'Rec (Recreation Ground).

Occasional malapropisms must not surprise us. These are awkward twists of words which jerk from a speaker unaware of them himself but to the amusement of hearers. Cumbrians have claimed to have had blood *confusions* and to have attended services of *conflammation;* after car crashes they have angrily demanded *condensation,* and attempting high-class business English they have asked to be kept *surprised of your letters.* Student Cumbrians, as I can personally testify, have in important examinations written about *Fraud* instead of *Freud* (more wisely than they know?) and quite often about *pronounciation.* Such travesties of language need a passing mention, just because they are so embarrassingly remembered.

Yet we must aim at a balanced picture. Certainly, if you insist on seeking the words out, you can find Cumbrians using words of all types and from almost every language under the sun—*joke* from Latin, *hara-kiri* meaning literally 'cut belly' from Japanese, *typhoon* 'big wind' from Chinese, etc., besides reduplications like *goody-goody* and *busybody,* echoic words like *flip-flops* for sandals, and slang such as *jaloppy* for their outworn vehicles that creak wearily from one M.O.T. test to another. Remember, however, that in Cumbria as in all English counties the mass of words is of native origin. Most of the short homely words like *yam* (home), *dooar* (door), *yak* (oak), etc. and most of the little 'link' words such as *and, but, to* and countless more are from Old English. Furthermore any word analysis would show that those used are less remarkable than they often sound, which in the interests of logic and general understanding is a good thing.

PLACE NAMES

History or legend appears in some of Cumbria's place names. *Dunmail Raise* is the most famous instance, perpetrating the name of the last king of Cumberland who, it is said, was killed by the Saxon monarch Edmund who raised a heap of stones over the corpse to mark the spot. *Wuffer* (Wolfa) is a farm in Great Salkeld parish, so-named from the tale of a wolf which was killed there many years ago.

Cumbrian place names often make better sense if you have some knowledge of Scandinavian. Thomas de Quincey wrote that Icelandic (which is a language developed from Old Norwegian) is the master key for local names and the dialect of Westmorland. He found that *Fairfield* comes from *faar* (sheep) plus *fald* (hill), Fairfield unlike its rocky neighbours being smooth and pastoral. *Watendlath* comes probably from three Norse words *vatn* (water), *endi* (end) and possibly *lar* (lair) to mean 'lair at the end of the lake'.

Scafell, invariably pronounced locally as Scawfell.
(Paul Chesmore)

It is certainly well tucked away in the hills just south of Derwentwater. A scrutiny of any map of Cumbria will reveal numbers of Old Norse words. Note especially those starting with the sound *sk-*, such as *scar* and *scree,* which cannot be from Anglo-Saxon which had no words beginning with that sound-combination.

Gaelic names are also much in evidence, especially for mountains; for example *Skidda* and nearby *Blencathra,* which sounds far more rugged than its English co-name *Saddleback.*

River names, too, are often Gaelic, but Anglo-Saxon and Scandinavian ones are also common. *Beck* is Scandinavian but is often combined with Anglo-Saxon names. Thus the Vale of Cartmel has a number of lively little streams with such down-to-earth names as *Clogger Beck, Middlefield Beck* and *Flow Beck* besides *Muddy Pool* and the strange-looking *Eea*, which is simply from Old English ea, meaning 'stream'. By contrast the river Derwent is named from Roman times, when it was *Derventio flumen.*

Different ways of pronouncing local place names are troublesome to the outsider. Every man believes that the way he pronounces the name of his native place is the best, and regards any BBC or other 'distortion' of it as a slur on his justifiable local pride. Time was when the spelling of a place name was known to only a few—the lord of the manor, the priest possibly, the parish clerk and the schoolmaster. Then things began to happen. Railways were built and stations had to have names; post offices were needed; compulsory schooling arrived with the 1870 Education Act. Now letters, postcards, telegrams and telephones reach the most isolated hamlet, and, though postcodes are forgotten, everyone must have an official address with its 'correct' spelling, which may be quite different from how the name is pronounced locally. This accounts for great differences like those below:

Spelt	**Spoken**	**Spelt**	**Spoken**
Ambleside	Ammelsat (referred to as **Amelsate** in the Rydal Boundary Roll, 1273)	Milnthorpe	Milnthrop
Aspatria	Speeatry	Northsceugh	Northscyoof
Bassenthwaite	Bassenthat	Penrith	Peerith (a pronunciation for at least the last 70 years)
Crossthwaite	Crossthat	Raughton Heah	Raffton Heed
Devoke Water	Devvack Watter	Scafell	Scawfell (though the BBC have pronounced it Scayfell)
Embleton	Emmelton	Sceugh Brow (near Penrith)	Sceeaf Brow
Faugh	Faff	Seaville	Seville
Gamblesby	Gammalby	Sebergham	Sebbaram
Greystoke	Greystick (Penrith-area pronunciation)	Sedbergh	Sebba
Haresceugh	Harescceaf	Skirwith	Skarrath (with two 'unstressed' vowels)
Hawkshead	Aakseyd	Staveley	Steeavla
Kirk Oswald	Kirkazzald	Ulpha	Qofer
Langwathby	Langanby	Ulverston	Ulverson or Oostan
Little Salkeld	Laal Saffel	Workington	Wukki'n
Maughenby	Maffenby	Wreay	Rare
Melmerby	Mellerby	Yeathouse	Yathouse or Yitass

Note: Occasionally there is a mispronunciation from misreading the spelling, like *Wonley* for Walney. Not many say this, but enough to be noticed.

A desire for prestige and love of the picturesque Lakeland terrain account for house names in other parts of Britain such as *Ambleside* or *Derwent*. The popularity of Lake District names has forced them onto addresses like *Eskdale Close* in Cardiff and whole housing estates in for example Macclesfield and Greater Manchester.

On the other hand, there is quite a large popularising trend which may have a long history if you go by examples such as *Pelter Bridge*, Rydal. This could be connected with *pell* (heavy rain) and the North Country expression 'It's peltin' down' (raining in torrents), since the river Rothay underneath it swells and rushes along after a heavy downpour. By this popularising tendency is not meant just the use of stock dialect words like *ootgang* for the way out for sheep etc. to the open fell, *lonnin'* for a lane, or *garth* for any little field connected with a farm, an orchard or a place where they keep a few hens. It affects more specific places, such as *t'watterin' gap* three and a half miles from Penrith to which beasts were herded to drink. Often the place names sound over-simplified, instances being *Back o' Shap* (behind Shap Fell) and *Back o' Skidda*. Another example of a simple name is *Top o' Lang Sneddle*, a valley up the Shap Road, where at Stockdale Farm was a farmer who would collect hay in November, *wid snaa on t'hay-cocks*.

At Gilcrux a salt water spring is called *Funny Tack,* incorporating a dialect word for 'taste' as in, 'This bacon has a queer tack'. A few hundred feet above Thirlmere hangs precariously the *Totty Stone,* tottering so unstably that it has received this playful name. Great Gable is known to mountaineers still fairly respectably as *The Gavel*; but on Gimmer Crag is the *mantelpiece* (the choice of word showing it is no brand new label), and above it what has been called the *young overhang* or the *thrutch* (Old English *þryccan*), because you have to push hard and move upwards fast before your arms weaken.

Indeed many places and other landmarks are better known by their nicknames. The Eskdale and Ravenglass Railway was re-named *Laal Ratty* by the dalesfolk as long ago as 1915. Kendal's Black Swan inn, in common with many another Black Swan, is *T'Mucky Duck.* The Travellers' Rest, 1,475 feet high on Kirkstone Pass and the fifth highest licensed premises in England, is known as *T'Jerry,* though it is not clear why.

Curious sayings attach themselves to places. 'Shap's where they shoe ducks', seems to have been vaguely true, though the wrong bird is mentioned. Geese from Ireland were, it seems, driven over tar and then made to walk through sand to given them protective 'footwear' for the journey east. A place *Goosegreen* is apparently named from this trade. Another old saying is 'fair as Irton pearls', from the time of Elizabeth I when the river Irt was famous for its stock of freshwater mussels in which exquisitely coloured mother-of-pearl is found Place names have all sorts of ramifications.

PERSONAL NAMES

People can receive nicknames from places. In Lakeland the most notorious are the *Borrowdal' Gowks,* from the story about the dalesmen who built the wall across the *Jaws of Borrowdal'* to retain the cuckoo; and the *Keswick Cushats* [Anglo-Saxon *cúscote* (wood-pigeon, ring-dove)], who were so named in retaliation presumably because Borrowdale stalwarts think Keswick people too soft.

Certain surnames are special to Cumbria. *Blamire, Moor* and

Mossop show the rugged nature of the terrain. Other local surnames are: (from Cumberland) Blencow, Cardew, Carlisle, Gillsland, Greystock, Hornsby, Mulcaster (i.e. Muncaster), Ousby, Ponsonby, Renwick: (from Westmorland) Bousfield, Brougham, Kendal, Lupton, Roskell (Rosegill), Sedgwick, Stockdale, Strickland: (from North Lancashire) Cartmell, Furness.

Packissons (Parkinsons) and Wilkissons (Wilkinsons) are very common in Barrow. However, over the years that town has seen important influxes from other parts of Britain. Many of its steel-makers and shipyard workers came from Staffordshire, Belfast and south of Glasgow. There were also Cornish tin-miners as indicated by Barrow surnames like *Trescatheric*. Millom, too, shows the influx of Cornish miners in surnames like Bowes, Peleymounter, Penaluna, Polglise, Spry and Barratt. In fact a mine-owner who moved there from Coniston was a Barratt. A strange story concerns two brothers of the same Cornish family who reached Millom. One spelt his name in the Cornish way Maddern and pronounced it with a West Country *r*; whilst the other, whose relatives still live there, spelt it *Maddran*, which Millom natives sound with a flapped *r*. The new pronunciation and spelling would be unheard of in Cornwall.

Finally Cumbrians have been endowed with their share of nicknames. Ted and Harold Walker, blacksmiths near Wordsworth's cottage, were known as *Eddard* and *Roidy* (few Harolds have their Christian names twisted like this.) William S. Atkinson, gamekeeper of Cunsey, was known as *Buckle* though he never knew why; and John Thompson Atkinson, driver of the Borrowdale bus, was far better known by the less imposing name of *John Ak*. Names, whether of local places or local people, are fascinating.

2. Cumbrian Writers

THE Lake District is associated with Wordsworth and his sister; Coleridge; Robert Southey and Thomas de Quincey, the essayist, who took over Dove Cottage after Wordsworth. People fall into the trap of thinking that Wordsworth, living at Grasmere and Rydal, spoke like an uneducated Lakelander and should therefore have filled his poems with dialect words, whereas his speech must have been that of an educated person and not too different from that of many a Cumbrian who is reading this book at the moment. Lengthy searches are needed before you find a dialect word in his pages. In his poem 'The Tables Turned', although he uses *throstle* (thrush), it is surrounded by non-dialect in the line, 'But hark! — how blithe the throstle sings!' No countryman would talk like that. In 'Mutability' he inserted *frosty rhyme* for hoar-frost, but merely to rhyme with *climb, chime, crime* and *sublime*. In 'Michael' he refers to the *brook*, never Cumbria's *beck*, although he does write of the *clipping tree*, using the Northern word for shearing. It seems quite anomalous that Wordsworth, so justly famous for his efforts to incorporate in his poetry 'the language of ordinary men' and, to my mind, in the highest class of poets, should make practically no use of dialect. It is one thing to try dialect writing and then perhaps discard it in order to reach the widest possible public: it is another to ignore it almost completely.

One of the Wordsworth stories to reach me concerns his ultra-conscientious, if not downright fussy efforts to polish his poems. As is well known, from 1813 to 1842 he was Stamp Distributor for Westmorland, with his office in Ambleside. The great-great-grandfather of one of my informants, who kept the sub post-office in Grasmere, had much trouble with the controller of stamps, who used to post letters and then demand them back to make alterations, which greatly worried the postmaster as it was against Post Office rules. His family used to declare, 'We'd rather have Coleridge come in drunk than Wordsworth sober.'

Dorothy Wordsworth was probably broader in speech than her brother. She uses some Lakeland words in her *Journals*, even though she spent many years away in London. Occasionally she uses a dialect word, such as *poke* for a bag or *skobbies* for chaffinches[1],

1. Vol. I, pp 90, 115 respectively.

as if it is very natural to her; but this is exceptional. She does include a fair amount of dialect, for example *sec* (such) as we have *ay* (yes), *calf-garth* (calf pen), *fra* (from), *gang* (go out), *clemmed* (starved); but usually when quoting from a rustic. Generally one feels that her Cumbrian dialect is accurate, but the interest is more that of a cultured outsider.

Of course geographical words like *ghyll* and *force* occur in the writings of the Wordsworths; but more of them used in a natural way, especially *fell* and *tarn*, appear in the works of Coleridge. As for the poet laureate Robert Southey, his chief local claim to our attention is apparently that from July 1818 to November 1819 he controlled *The Westmorland Gazette*, that important paper which in modern times has for example printed Wainwright's extremely useful guides to the fells, and Southey's 'head' adorned the paper's stationery until a year or two ago.

Charles Dickens, despite his main reputation as a close observer of Victorian London and the South East, also had links with Cumbria. In the autumn of 1857 he and Wilkie Collins made a Lake District tour to gather material for a series of articles in *Household Words*. These duly appeared under the title 'The Lazy Tour of Two Idle Apprentices'. He was particularly amazed at Wigton, where, though trade was negligible, he could nevertheless see from his hotel window five drapers' shops, with a sixth next door and just round the corner five more. What is most commendable about Dickens is that, though an *off-comer* in the North-West, he had travelled a long and perhaps uncomfortable distance to research his material himself. You cannot beat authenticity, and it shows that even a writer of genius depends on making quite certain of many seemingly insignificant points of fact.

Every writer cannot be mentioned, but we must include here Hugh Walpole, writer of *The Herries Chronicle*; whilst Beatrix Potter who lived at Sawrey, through her delightful tales of Peter Rabbit and his friends, has become very much a local institution.

In Cumbrian dialect literature, as E.R. and M. Denwood have carefully pointed out[1], the first recorded poet of any note is the Reverend Josiah Relph (1712-43), who was born at Sebergham and after education at Appleby School and Glasgow University returned to his native village as schoolmaster. He was a very minor poet, almost unknown except to the student of dialect verse. His work is based on classical models.

Then came two other minor writers. Ewan Clark (1734-1811) published his longest poem, 'The Rustic', when he was seventy; his best-known song is 'I trudg'd up to Lunnon'. Charles Graham (1761-1789) of Penrith wrote, so far as we can tell, only one dialect poem, a dialogue 'Gwerdy and Will', but it is full of genuine

1. In the introduction to **Oor Mak o' Toak** (see bibliography).

Cumbrian humour.

Miss Susanna Blamire (1747-1794), born near Dalton, was in quite a different class. She was nationally famous for her Scottish lyrics, but her Cumbrian verse is also very highly thought of, though the best of it was done in collaboration. She excels in pathos and sly humour. If she has a defect, it is in not portraying the rougher elements of Cumbrian life, but then how many writers even today dare put into their books samples of all they hear or see? Miss Catherine Gilpin (1738-1811), her collaborator, was born at Scaleby Castle near Carlisle and for some time lived together with Miss Blamire in that city. Her output of dialect verse was small but of good quality.

Still basing some of our remarks on the Denwoods' fine summary, we turn to Cumbrian dialect writers contemporary with Wordsworth and the Romantic Revival, although their works unlike those of Wordsworth, Shelley, Scott and Burns show little trace of romance. These dialect writers may all be considered minor ones. Mark Lonsdale (1758-1815), born in Carlisle the son of a blacksmith,

Susanna Blamire, born near Dalton in 1747, was a famed Cumbrian lyricist.

wrote numerous songs for the plays he produced at Sadler's Wells Theatre and the Theatre Royal, Drury Lane; but his dialect fame rests on his boisterous poem 'The Upshot' full of droll humour and lifelike characterisation. John Stagg (1770-1823), Robert Anderson (1770-1833) and John Rayson (c. 1803-1859) had all very sad aspects to their lives. It is to be hoped that misery is not the main qualification for becoming a poet. Stagg, the Blind Bard, died at Workington in a common lodging-house. He was educated for the Church, but near-blindness forced him into other occupations, even the running of a bookshop at Wigton. Anderson, a victim of drink, died at Carlisle in abject poverty. He left many rough and boisterous ballads and songs, but few to excite tender sympathy except 'Reed Robin' and 'King Roger'. He lacks the human touch and kindly humour of, for example, the dialect poets famous in Lancashire, Sam Laycock and Edwin Waugh ('Ned Waff'). Rayson failed in business in both Carlisle and London before turning schoolmaster. His best poem is perhaps 'Ann o' Hethersgill'.

In the next phase, Cumbrian dialect writing really begins to flower. A.C. Gibson (1813-74), the son of a sea-captain and best known as author of the 1869 *Folk Speech of Cumberland*, became a doctor who practised around Coniston. His prose and poetry are, however, rather too polished and artificial. Far superior to Gibson's were the prose and verse of John Richardson (1817-86). He was a waller who became a teacher in the very school that he himself had built!—such versatility might be very useful nowadays. He portrayed characters well and had an inside knowledge of Cumbrian life, especially of the farming community. His two volumes of *Cummerland Talk* accurately show the life of a mid-nineteenth century dalesman. William Dickinson wrote *Cumbriana*, a book of sketches and anecdotes and his 1859 *Glossary of Words and Phrases of Cumberland*. His works are still eagerly sought; and he did much to preserve the dialect and the memory of old Cumberland customs. The Reverend Thomas Ellwood, besides important work on Scandinavian etymologies, wrote some good dialect verse. Stanley Martin, better known as 'Gwordie Greenup' (b. 1846) was a bank clerk in Cockermouth and later in Penrith who printed three dialect works including his fine poem 'A Howth-Gill Hero'. The brothers John Denwood Junior (1871-1917) and J.M. Denwood (1869-1933) are famous for their *Canny Oald Cummerland* (1910), *Shepherds' Meet* (1913) and *Idylls of a North Countrie Fair* (1916). All their books, as in life, mix humour, pathos and realism.

Dorothy Una Ratcliffe was an enthusiastic writer whose poems are full of local words. She was prominent in the Cumbrian Literary Group of the Yorkshire Dialect Society, and is perhaps best remembered for the quiet help she gave to many an aspiring dialect author on both sides of the Pennines. Graham Sutton of Keswick was a well-known Lakeland novelist. Enid Wilson is a native writer who occasionally uses the odd dialect word. Margaret Cropper, in her nineties now, has done another book of poems. Dudley Hoys, who settled in Eskdale after Army service, has written extensively about Lakeland, besides finding time to develop a lifelong interest in farming. His books are very stimulating.

A famous name is that of Melvyn Bragg. He writes less dialect now, perhaps because like other writers he has to be intelligible to a mass of the population, but he has a genuine 'feel' for things local. He makes his country people talk in quite an acceptable way. Equally high on the list must surely go Norman Nicholson, well-known as a Cumbrian poet for at least a quarter of a century and important too as a prose writer and editor of a most instructive Lakeland anthology. He still lives in the house where he was born, and has a passionate interest in anything from the Millom area in particular and Cumbria in general.

Cumbria has not had the great number of famous writers that for example Lancashire, Yorkshire or the Home Counties can boast. More is the pity! Yet it has had, and continues to have, some excellent ones. It seems invidious to single out a few modern writers, but it will be realised that only lack of space prevents mentioning others and that it is better to make a start with some names than mention none at all.

A snag is that dialect almost ceases to be dialect when you become intensely aware of it. A little while ago there took place in Cumbria a children's dialect-writing competition. Its idea was good—to foster a love of language in the rising generation—but the aim was not properly achieved. Entries showed children using exactly the words they would have used in ordinary English, but in comic spelling. This is not dialect writing.

Who, then, writes true dialect? Two types of people—the educated who can bring to bear a scientifically accurate but also a sympathetic approach, and those who speak it all day long and write it down naturally to the best of their ability. These latter never use the word *dialect,* just saying, 'That's the way we speak,' but from them comes much of the best dialect poetry. If you belong to either class, you will be warmly appreciated.

Fortunately Cumbria is the home of the thriving and enthusiastic Lakeland Dialect Society, founded in 1939 and second oldest of the three in England. (The others are The Yorkshire Dialect Society, founded in 1904, and Lancashire's Dialect Society. Strange that for example no Cockney, Lincolnshire or Devonshire Dialect Society has so far blossomed!). The Lakeland Dialect Society holds three or four meetings annually in different parts of the county, including every two years a dialect service. These simple services are much enjoyed by large congregations of members and local people. From the 1972 service, held at Ambleside Methodist Church, here first is the Lord's Prayer:

'Oor Father, which art in heeven, Halled be thy neam; Thy Kingdom cum; Thy will be dean; in earth as 'tis in heevan. Gie us this day oor daily breed. An' forgive us oor trespasses, as we forgive them thet trespass ageanst us. An' lead us nut inta temptation. But deliver us fra evil: For thine ist Kingdom, t'Poor, an t'Gloory, For ivver and ivver. Amen.'

Now follow two of the dialect hymns

Tune: Aurelia

Yance Mair we're met togither
Frae Cumbrian dale and fell
Auld frens and new combinin'
Thy Praises, Lord, to tell;
No accents high or mighty
But prayer with humble soond
That our old speech may prosper,
Mid changes all aroond.

We bless Thee Lord for't many,
Whese neames we divvent ken,
'At handit doon oor language
Fra times 'ats lang, lang sen
The torch may we keep burnin'
In story, verse and sang ...
Seea them 'at follo' efter
Can carry it alang.

Ooor Saviour cracked wid t'shipherds
An' fwolk ev low degree:
He suffert for us sinners
An' hung on Calvery's Tree.
May we, frae His example,
Larn meekness still today
Yet catch that glimpse o' Glory
That cannot pass away.

J.T.R.

Tune: Crimond

The Lord's mi Sheppert, Ah'll nut want;
He maks meh doon teh bide
In pasters green; He leadeth meh
Bih t' quiet watter-side.

Mi sowl He doth restore ageann,
An' meh teh walk doth mak
Widdin t' paths ev righteousness,
E'en fer His own neamm's seakk.

Aye, though Ah walk in deeth's dark deall,
Yit will Ah fear nee ill;
Fer thoo art wid meh, an' thih rod
An' staff meh comfort still.

Mi teable Thoo hest funished
In presence ev mi foes;
Mi heed Thoo dost wid oil anoint,
An' mi cup ow'rflows.

Goodness an' marcy aw mi life
'll surely follow meh.
An' in God's Hoose fer ivvermair
Mi dwelling-pleace 'll be.

Of course the thoughts expressed in the hymns are what mattered most, but helping them considerably were the music and the dialect. This appears a legitimate and by no means irreverent use of dialect writing.

Finally we must consider dialect writings intended chiefly for the student and scholar. Over the centuries many local glossaries have been compiled and published in books and newspaper articles. Some are important, others less so. Amongst the most significant are those listed at the start of Chapter 8. The first major academic breakthrough, however, occurred in 1889, with the publication by the Early English Text Society of A.J. Ellis's *Early English Pronunciation, Part V,* and its abridgment the following year, again for the Society, under the title *English Dialects—their Sounds and Homes.*

Ellis, England's first truly great phonetician, divided the country into 32 dialect areas putting all Cumberland, Westmorland, northwest Yorkshire and 'Lancashire north of the sands' into area 31, apart from territory east and north-east of Carlisle, which he placed with Northumberland in area 32. He states in his abridgment (page 113), 'The country is full of hills and lakes, and the dialect seems to be in an older form than that of D 30 (his area covering most of Yorkshire). It is probably the old history of the emigrant language remaining practically what it was at the time of emigration, while the parent speech has changed.' Compare in this respect Quebeqois, which French Canadians fiercely uphold, with modern French. Ellis continues, 'To comparatively recent times, as the name Cumberland shows, these countries were inhabited by the Celtic Cymry, and were conquered by Northumbrians from Yorkshire. Very possibly

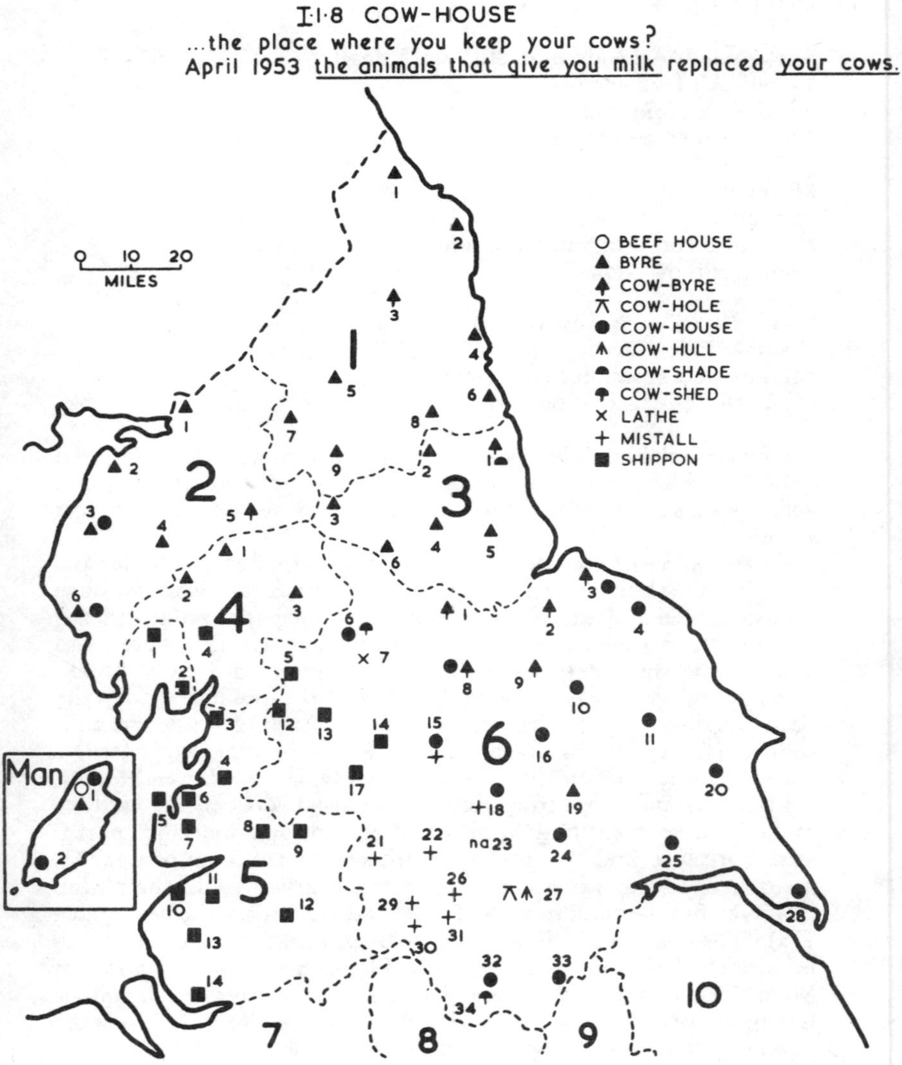

Map from the Leeds University Survey of English Dialects showing the various north of England expressions for a cow-house: in Cumbria a 'byre', 'cow-byre' or 'shippon'.

therefore they retained the language of the time of conquest for an appreciable time.' Although he states, 'The general character of all D 31 is so like Variety I (his variety from round Craven and the north-west Yorkshire dales) that this may be taken as the type of the district', of his six specimens he admits (p.115) that the Keswick variety was 'presenting many difficulties' and states that Variety VI from Abbey Holme in north-west Cumberland, unlike the rest of the area, had *ey* generally in words whose standard Middle English form had ī such as *like* and *ride*.

In 1904 appeared Joseph Wright's *English Dialect Dictionary*, a landmark in dialect collection whose six volumes should be available in every larger reference library. It was compiled second-hand from local glossaries etc., including information gathered by A.J. Ellis and his helpers. Inevitably it has a few omissions and has been mildly criticised (for example for including words like *ramshackle* which most people now would class as ordinary English), but it does give a very good picture of what dialect terms were alive in those days. Yet the localities are not too closely defined. If you want to know whether a particular word or pronunciation was current in 1904, you can easily check it in this dictionary; but it might be marked *mCum* 'mid-Cumberland', *wWm* 'west Westmorland' or even just *NCy* 'North Country' and certainly not as precisely as for example Brampton or Underbarrow, which can be done on modern dialect maps. The last volume of the dictionary includes Joseph Wright's *English Dialect Grammar,* which was also published separately. It is comparatively short and not as imposing as the massive lexical side of his work; but then, I am shocked to report, few people have an undying fascination for grammar, standard or otherwise, and he would have to consider what was most wanted.

Monographs on particular dialects are normally very useful. In 1906 T.O. Hirst wrote his *Grammar of the Dialect of Kendal* (*Westmorland*) and in 1913 B. Brilioth followed with the *Grammar of the Dialect of Lorton* (*Cumberland*). These scientific contributions led in 1927 to P.H. Reaney's important *Grammar of the Dialect of Penrith.* He used a very sound method of gathering and checking information. He explains (pp. vii-viii), 'For more than eighteen months after I had begun collecting my material no-one in Penrith except two or three intimate friends—certainly no dialect speaker—knew of my intentions. My method was to ramble round the district taking every opportunity of conversing with or listening to the conversations of natives. Market days, sales of farm stock and agricultural implements, and Saturday evenings in village inns, all enabled me to hear the dialect spoken naturally and without affectation.... When I had collected a fair amount of material, I verified it with the aid of several natives of Penrith.' He adds that about one twelfth of the vocabulary came from the Norse settlers, and that the romance element, on his calculations about a seventh

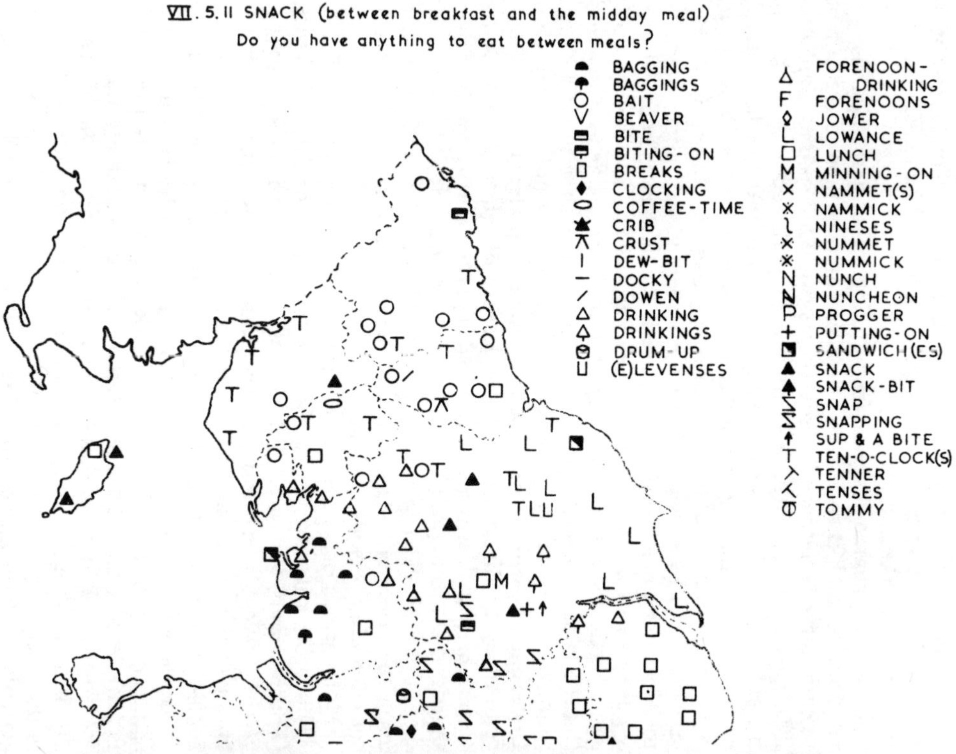

Alternative Cumbrian expressions for a snack (between breakfast and the midday meal) are 'ten-o-clocks', 'coffee-time' and 'bait'. The map is from the Leeds University Survey of English Dialects.

of the words collected, included a number such as *fash* (trouble), *mel* (mallet), *sehm* (lard) and *stooary* (dusty) which were not found in the literary language.

Equally systematic have been university dissertations on the speech of particular villages. The first for Cumbria, and a very good one, was Mabel G. Round's 1952 M.A. dissertation for Leeds University on the dialect of Broughton-in-Furness, with an important section dealing with terms from its basket-making industry. Until the creation of the University of Lancaster, however, Cumbria was handicapped by not having such an institution on its doorstep, and consequently research of this type has been limited.

A giant step forward in dialect investigation was the Leeds *Survey of English Dialects,* started under Professors Orton and Dieth in 1949, with about 1800 carefully framed questions to be answered in about 300 English localities. This was originally planned as a three-pronged venture; Oxford University to survey the South of England, Leeds the North and Edinburgh to be responsible for Scotland. In the first few months Oxford University unfortunately had to drop out and, although Professor McIntosh of Edinburgh visited Leeds for liaison purposes, the Scottish survey, whose maps were published in 1978, had to work under different conditions and initially relied very much on correspondence. With hindsight, it is easy to say that greater collaboration would have helped even more, but it was splendid that against financial obstacles the Edinburgh and Leeds surveys got off the ground at all. So far as Cumbria is concerned it was well served, for all the twelve chosen places (six in Cumberland, four in Westmorland and two in what was then North Lancashire) were investigated by a very experienced interviewer, Stanley Ellis. His results are extremely reliable and you can ask no more.

Switzerland has long had an interest in Cumbrian speech, Switzerland with its high mountains and sharp valleys being similarly riddled with dialects. In 1952 Dr. Fritz Rohrer of Zurich, now known for his books and tapes on English, mapped what is called the Northern-North Midland border, an important line distinguishing various historical groups of words, such as Northern *eeat* (eat) and *man* from North Midland *eyt* and sometimes *mon.* It was in Cumbria that his Renault car crashed, when at the last moment he had to avoid some *bairns.* Those who saw the total wreck wondered how he had escaped alive: dialect-hunting has its perils. In 1966 Professor E. Kolb of Bern produced his *Phonological Atlas of the Northern Region,* including what is now Cumbria and basing his beautifully clear maps on the Leeds University results; and in 1973 one of his pupils Willy Elmer, working chiefly from an inshore-fishing questionnaire that I had devised, went round the English and Welsh coasts, including Cumbria's, to produce his book *The Terminology of Fishing...,* remarkable amongst other things for its detailed explanations of objects and processes, and for its photographs.

A further development in recent years has been the making of tapes by the University of Lancaster from elderly Barrow natives; and currently work under Dr. Widdowson of the University of Sheffield is in progress for the *Atlas Linguarum Europae,* the Atlas of European Languages, whereby responses from four Cumbrian places will be compared not only with others from England but those from the rest of Europe. The localities chosen were Great Strickland and Staveley (of old Westmorland), and Brigham and Abbeytown (formerly in Cumberland). Because of the larger mesh of this European survey's network, no place in old Lancashire north of the sands has been selected. This time, for reasons of economy and convenience, the four places were investigated by four different field workers, which is not ideal; but they were all well trained and experienced. The questionnaire used is, at least in my opinion, a delight to work with, chiefly because of its many pictures, although naturally a few of the notions do not apply to England. As all four places were investigated also by the Leeds survey, it will be interesting to see how their dialects have changed in the last twenty five years or so.

Thus, both in more general authorship and for specific work on dialect, Cumbria has been helped by a good many distinguished and scholarly writers. Even more important, it is still the home of hard-working, popular and famous authors, and of people with an abiding interest in its speech. This must lead to its further literary renown, and to dialect meetings of wide appeal and worthy scholarship. Cumbrian writings are alive and well, rejoicing in the past but ready to serve readers of today. Here lies the recipe for their success.

3. Cumbrian Sounds

IN his *Dictionary of Archaic and Provincial Words,* written in 1847, J.O. Halliwell somewhat rashly states (p.xiii), 'The dialects of Cumberland, Westmorland, Northumberland and Durham may be considered to be identical in all essential peculiarities.' He does qualify this by remarking upon 'the chief differences arising from the mode of pronunciation', but surely wide differences, like the Cumbrian flapped *r* compared with the throated uvular *r* of the 'Northumbrian burr' (which I have seen attributed to the quality of Northumbrian soil!), suggest fundamentally different dialects. Admittedly Halliwell was writing long ago, but we must certainly check whether all English dialects north of about Lancaster and Middlesbrough can be grouped under one head.

First, however, a warning must be given that, although Cumbria rejoices in some marvellously intriguing sounds, it is quite impossible to show them exactly in writing. It is widely believed that phonetic alphabets can do it. A.J. Ellis, the nineteenth century mathematician and dialectologist, invented one, which he called paleotype. He had an accurate ear and, aided by the explanations in the introductions to his works, I believe I can infer roughly the sounds meant, but would still be most grateful for an accurate translation into modern phonetic symbols (Here is a splendid scope for a student-researcher).

Another such alphabet was invented by Melville Bell and adapted by Sweet, from whom George Bernard Shaw took ideas to create Professor Higgins of his play *Pygmalion,* which was made into the musical *My Fair Lady*. Other alphabets were devised by Lepsius, Meinhof, and Otto Jesperson, who in his *Essentials of English Grammar* was already in the 1930s using speech symbols later developed by the International Phonetic Association. It is truly surprising that this internationally used system is not better known. Only recently, in question time at a meeting of a very interested and knowledgeable society, I was asked whether I ever used phonetics; and when I wrote in phonetics on the blackboard the resulting questions asked there were wide open mouths as if it was another wonder of the world. Again, the Simplified Spelling Society (founded 1908), whose patron is the Duke of Edinburgh, is continually making strenuous efforts to persuade us to write words like the combinations of sounds inside them, so that for example, the Bible might start, 'In THe bigining woz the wurd and THe wurd woz with God'.

All these systems are admirable, but they all partially fail because speech can never be written down perfectly. Yet it can be shown more accurately in a scientific script, so please do not grumble too much if you do not follow every vowel nuance in this book, where for the convenience of the majority of readers examples have to be shown in modified spelling. If you need more accuracy, seek a phonetic translation or tape-recordings. Better still, if you want the real thing, keep listening direct to Cumbrians themselves.

That said, there is still a great deal that books can usefully show us about Cumbrian sounds. In short vowels, there is a noticeably high *ɪ*, rather like a short *ee* and reminiscent of the type heard in the North Riding and County Durham, and by Frenchmen who have no *ɪ*- sound but are determined to learn 'Eengleesh'. An historical *a* before *ng* still typically remains *a* in Cumbria, so that we find complaints like, 'Ah's nut strang (not strong)', 'It's ower lang (too long)', 'He's spelt it wrang, iv'ry word'. There is some *u* for Standard English sound *ɪ* after rounded initial consonants; for example *whup* (whip), *shuppon* (shippon), 'What's t'matter, Wulla (Willy)?'.

Long vowels show most interesting developments. Words from Middle English long *ā*, such as *late, name* and *gable*, yield a variety of pronunciations. For example Cumbrians prefer not to call a spade a spade, with a slightly diphthongised *ay*-sound as in Standard English. They employ one of the variants below. Type one is preferred in the remote eastern farming districts, types two and three are intermediate, type four is a favourite in South Cumbria, whilst types five and six are approximations to Standard English:

Example	**Vowel in phonetics**	**Vowel explained**
1. spee-erd	ɪə	rhyming with **here**
2. spyad + speead	ja ɪa	with **a** as in Italian **mama** mi**a**
3. spay-ad	ea	tense **ay** + Italian **a**
4. spay-erd	eə	tense **ay** + unstressed central vowel
5. spehd	ɛ:	like a long **e** as in **get**
6. spayd	e:	like the French tense **ays** in **bébé**

The modern vowel from Middle English e̲[1] in some parts, for example in the speech of Tom Richardson who has farmed 40 years around Caldbeck, is consistently diphthongised towards əɪ, so that 'See these green fields' would sound like 'Ser-ee ther-eese grer-een fer-eelds'. More often in Cumbrian it resembles *ee*. For the vowel in words such as *white* and *time*, Northern Cumbria often uses *ey*, for that is where you find for example *seyd* (side), *leyce* (lice) and *meyce* (mice).

Middle English $\bar{o}^1$, which occurred in words now spelt with *oo* such as *noon, moon, boots* and *tooth,* has normally given rise to a threefold development, namely:

	Phonetically	Example
1. Traditional **ee-er**	ɩ ə	**mee-ern** (moon)
2. Intermediate **i-u**	ɩ ω	in West Cumbria **mi-un**
3. Approximate Standard English **oo**	u:	especially in South Cumbria **moon.**

There is also a striking fourth development, noticeable from elderly informants from around Kendal, who say, for example, 'Thoo's nut ganna dyer it (You're not going to do it)' pronouncing their 'do' like French *dieu* with its rounded vowel. The same people will say, 'Git thi byerts (boots) on. Gaa ootseyd, there's a full myern (moon)'; and at Christmas dinner, 'Dig thi tyerth (tooth) into that gyers (goose)'. This vowel is very like that recorded by the Leeds *Survey of English Dialects* from nearby County Durham.

Middle English $\bar{o}^2$, which has normally brought words now spelt with *oa* or *o* + consonant + *e,* yields historical *ee-er,* phonetically ɩ ə, as in *spee-erks* (spokes), *bee-erth* (both), *clee-ers* (clothes). *Fee-erl* (foal) has also been collected. This last pronunciation needs watching, because I was once sent to a North Riding farm to check another fieldworker's collection of it which my bosses disbelieved — with reason, as it happened, since the fieldworker concerned, who was from overseas, for misunderstanding something the farmer had said, had been called jokingly 'a bloody feeal (fool)'. However, as it was Stanley Ellis who gathered the pronunciation in Cumbria and it certainly fits the possible patterns of Cumbria's $\bar{o}^2$, it will doubtless be correct. Needless to say, in a dialect situation so sensitive to modern change and influence of the standard language, there are other types of variants for example:
ya or *i-a* comes quite often in *yak* (oak), *yam* (home); and sometimes in *bi-ath* (both);
ye or *i-e* appears in *yek* (oak) and *bi-eth* (both) in West Cumbria;
ay-a is found in *bay-ath* (both) and *clay-az* (clothes) in South Cumbria;
and *oo-a* in *nooat* (note), *vooat* (vote) etc. over the whole county.
No wonder the dialectologist has a frustrating task!

Words from Middle English $\bar{u}$, like *house, how* and *cloud,* give an *oo*-type vowel in the north of the region, and *ow* in the south; whilst the Middle English dipthong *au* intermittently gives *aa,* so you may hear about conditions in December, 'I saa it snaa'. Thus Cumbrian stressed vowels show plenty of variety.

Consonants also are interesting in Cumbria. Let us start with five sounds or combinations of sounds over which there is little dispute, namely initial and final *k,* final *g, l, r* and medial *d.* The initial and final *ch* of Standard English is often represented by *k.* Thus Carlisle Cathedral is familiarly *Big Kirk,* and a common sight until recent years was that of farmers' *kerns* (churns) awaiting collection at *t'end o't'lonnin*. If you went *doon t'lonnin*, you might conceivably pass silver *birks* (birch trees) before reaching the farm at threshing time to see *kaff* (chaff) being separated from the corn. Hanging in the farmhouse might be a *flick* (flitch) of bacon. Similarly, instead of the *-dge* expected in Standard English at word-ends, we hear *-g* to produce *brigs* for bridges and *rigs* for the ridges in a ploughed field.

Cumbria's *l* sound is a very light one, lighter than the Irish *l* and of course very different from the Cockney dark *l* which sometimes verges on *u*. After back vowels it can disappear, as, for example, in *waw* (wall) and the strange-sounding *woo* (wool). The region's *r*, unlike that of all other English counties, is often a flapped one; i.e. the tongue starts moving as for a Scottish 'rolled' *r* but touches the roof of the mouth only once. After *t* (which in this case is what is called a 'dental' one, sounding more like *th*), the flapped *r* is especially noticeable. Thus, for example, *trees* sounds rather like *threes* and *tread* like *thread*. Another striking consonantal difference is *d* for voiced *th* medially in a word or sentence, as in *nayder* (neither), *wid four legs* or the comparison *as leet as a fedder*.

Now we turn to consonants where the picture is less clear. They are initial *h*, what results in words spelt with *q-*, and an apparently gratuitous sound *w*. In the northern half of Cumbria, as in Northumberland and North America, initial *h-* is retained. Writers imitating the speech of Northern Cumbria do not drop their *h*s. Indeed its retention in the county is fairly wide: country girls from around Millom, for instance, keep their *h*s. Yet around Kendal it is sometimes dropped and farther south this is regular. Dropping of *h* is frequent in common words like *how* and *him*: in those with an educated or scientific bias, like *haulage* or *helicopter*, where the speaker tends to be on his better linguistic behaviour, it is rare. Dropping the *h* conflicts with Standard English to cause uncertainty, generating confusions like 'a howl (owl) in 'Arry's chimla' or threats like 'Yon himpident feller needs "ullin"' —*Hullin'*, locking overnight in a *pig-hull* or pig-sty, was an old Upper Eden Valley method of *learnin' forriners* (teaching strangers) not to court and poach a village's pretty lasses.

As for initial letter *q-*, B. Kirkby writing in 1898 (*Lakeland Words*) states, 'In our dialect, words with Q in them are subject to evasion, or that letter is substituted by some other.' His examples include *wharteren* (quartern), *white* (quite), *whart* (quart), *whist* (quiet), *whent* (quaint), *wharl* (quarry), *whench* (quench), *which* (quick) and its combinations *whicksilver* (quicksilver), *whicksand* (quicksand) and *whick-set* (quick-set). All these seem to have arisen from a strongly voiced initial aspirate, phonetically X w and like the Scottish 'voiceless wh', being thought to resemble the sound of letter *q*. However Kirkby himself admits that an alternative for 'quench' is *slocken*, a word I find still alive and in Carlisle with a guttural fricative X for the spelling *ck*. Of his examples listed above, the only two I have so far noted are *whick* in the meaning 'alive' and (with a different pronunciation) *Wisht!* for '(Be) Quiet!' The great-uncle of one of my informants used to shout it when squabbling children interrupted him in the delicate and dangerous operation of shaving by cut throat razor.

Kirkby's other examples are *swirt* or *sooart* (squirt), *thwacker* (quaker), *twinzy* (quinsey), *twill* (quill) and *twilt* (quilt), which all involve attempts to sound letters *qu*. Kirkby continues about his examples, 'Some of these are no doubt merely humorous variations, but the bulk of them are permanent in the folk speech.' This argument seems very doubtful on the first matter and untrue on the second. Firstly, some may be childish and of the *little/likkle* type, but all may be genuine attempts at the sounds. Secondly, the dialectal position has so vastly changed in the eighty years since he wrote that one would have great difficulty in using them all today. The examples ring true, but they are examples from the distant past.

The other debatable matter about consonants is whether a *w*-sound follows that of *k* in words like *coal, coat* and *folk*. J.O. Halliwell in the introduction to his 1847 *Dictionary* wrote, 'In Cumberland, *wo* is in frequent use instead of the long *o*,' but follows with a ballad whose only 'example' is *scwornin* (scorning). There are genuine traces of such a *w* in the Leeds linguistic atlas recordings, notably *cwoal* and *cwoat* from Abbeytown and Brigham; but some modern Lakeland writers native to the area are themselves surprised to see some of their fellow authors still so fond of it, writing for example *fwolk* (folk) for what is now generally pronounced *fouk*, i.e. with *o* plus *u* vowels but no *w*. Here again, and rather like the old literary convention of Victorian Cockney before George Bernard Shaw and others came onto the scene, the old dialect seems to have changed faster than writers may admit.

Lastly, what shall we say about the glottal stop, that sound like a little cough masquerading as a *t* in words like *pi'y* (pity) and *Wukki'n* (Workington)? Some would reply, 'The less said, the better.' They brand the glottal stop as 'harsh, lazy, ungainly, horrible'; but these are risky value judgments because the poor glottal stop is only a sound, and one that is a standard feature of some languages such as German. However, keeping to factual reporting, it is noted here that the glottal stop has reached Cumbria, most strikingly in the speech of youngsters in Barrow, where it has probably spread from Lancashire towns. To a smaller extent it is reaching the younger generation of Whitehaven and Workington, but has not spread to rural districts. In fact, compared with most English shires (outstanding among which in this respect is County Durham) and cities (for example *Brum*, Leicester and above all London), Cumbria is still fairly free of the glottal stop. That to many teachers seems a comfort, though increasing opportunity to travel may shortly bring it in greater numbers.

To summarise, through its more isolated position on the map Cumbria's special choices of vowels and consonants are likely to persist for quite some time. longer than their counterparts in most other English shires. On that note of qualified optimism this review of their salient features ends.

4. General and Rural Dialect

GRAMMAR, INTONATION AND SPEED OF UTTERANCE

THESE need discussing first because they are the framework on which words, pronunciations and meanings hang. Grammar is particularly vital, for without it words have no connected sense. Some maintain that broad-spoken Cumbrians have abolished grammar, but this can never be. Their grammar may be highly unorthodox but it is still grammar, the type most fitted to their variety of language.

Gender, at least, is logical. Boats, cars and tools are *it*: absent is the enthusiast's affectionate *she* for his boat or car—Cumbrians are made of sterner stuff— and they have nothing akin to the childish-sounding *he* for a heavy tool, formerly used in parts of the West Country. As in most other English dialects, after numbers nouns of quantity usually remain singular; for example 'ivvery six month', 'five mile up', 'He was six foot'. As in Yorkshire, 'the' is represented by *t,* for example 'There's t'libary (the library)'.

In verbs, the retention of *-s* throughout the present tense ('Ah knows it', 'They misses their friends') is characteristically Northern. The dialect has far fewer strong verbs than in the list of about 250 in J. Wright's *Old English Grammar* but still significantly more than the 90 or so of current Standard English. It also has much more variety, such as: 'Look what he's wrote (written)', 'I come (came) yesterday', 'We've spoke (spoken) agin that', 'Noo, look what thoo's brekken (broken)!'; and very commonly uses *gitten,* such as in 'Asta gitten yan?' (Have you got one?). Some odd uses of the verb *to go* have been noted; for instance by Norman Nicholson 'You won't can go' from Whitehaven, and *went* which he has heard once or twice in Workington and Whitehaven for the infinitive as in 'You won't can went'. *Mud* for 'might' is another verbal peculiarity. A Kendal-district farmer told me of his hay, 'It'll nut fire, but it mud mould'.

In pronouns, '-self' becomes the Northern *-sell,* sometimes in unnecessarily reflexive use as 'I'll sit misell', 'Gan(go)an' wash thisell'. *Thoo* for singular 'you' is common, especially in emphatic positions as when an informant airily told me about his *shuppon,* 'Thoo would call it a cow-shed.' Like Yorkshire's, the relative for 'which' or 'who' is *at:* 'Them pigs at (which) we kept', 'The fowk at (who) lives next dooar'. Sometimes this relative is omitted; for example 'There was an aal feller used (who used) to gaan oot wid us'.

The prepositional phrase *for to* occurs, such as in 'for to (in order to) peel it'; and adverbs differ from Standard English a good deal. Note particularly *happen* and *mebbe* (perhaps); *aye* (yes) but in Barrow also occasional *yer*; *ower* (too) (rhyming with Standard English *our*) as in 'It's ower clarty (too muddy) doon theer'; *that* (so) as in 'not that many dresses'; and *nobbut*, as in 'I've nobbut selt yan (sold only one)'.

Intensifying adverbs include *varra* and *right*, for example, 'Be varra/right quick', but the great favourite is *gay* or *gaily*. Examples are: 'It's gay wick (very lively)', 'in gay good fettle (in very good condition)'. By now you will be *gay thrang* (very busy) probing this Cumbrian grammar and I confidently expect you are doing *gaily weel* (very well), enough to realise that *gaily* by omission of the verb can serve almost as an adjective, such as in the greeting *Are you gaily*? (Are you keeping well?).

A number of quaint grammatical usages of the area appear to have become extinct. One is *at* for 'to' before the infinitive, as in *summat at eyt* (something to eat), a type recorded in 1890 for South Westmorland and Furness.[1] Others now apparently lost to oblivion, though current in 1905, are *all their* (all of them) and *which* for people, as in the Lord's Prayer, 'Our Father, which art in heaven...[2]. Thus make of it what you will, but there is the grammatical skeleton of living Cumbrian dialect.

Intonation draws comments from my helpers that it is 'more musical and flexible in Borrowdale', 'twines on more in Grasmere', has 'a still leveller tone in Kendal'. That is, the more rural the community, the greater the general rise and fall of the voice. This agrees so far with my impressions and mechanical recordings from the Lake District, but readers' views on this little-researched subject would be very welcome.

Urban speech is usually somewhat quicker than rural, though there are many exceptions. The speech of, say, Workington is more slurred than that of the surrounding countryside, and Barrow's faster than Workington's. A Barrow native was reported to me as almost unintelligible to his *marrers* (workmates) in the Workington steel mills, partly because of his words but chiefly through his rapid speech. Village speech, as a rule, is in contrast very condensed, saving words and in the process giving the few selected greater prominence. For example *Aa's gaan in t'bank* means 'I am going to cut my way down across the breast of the hill'—six words or parts of them instead of fourteen.

1. Ellis, A.J., **English Dialects, their Sounds and Homes,** p.113.
2. Wright, J., **English Dialect Grammar,** paras 410, 422.

GREETINGS, SENTENCE-FILLERS AND FAREWELLS

These are other interesting features of language in this part of the North West. Greetings are of various types, from the formulaic 'How do?' to those inviting definite replies such as: 'A ya gaily?' (Are you all right?) -answer 'Gaily weel' (quite well); 'Wheresta gaan?' - 'A's gan yam' (I'm going home); 'Hoo's thissell?' (How are you?); 'Where's thoo come frae?'. Some invite blunt replies: for example 'Ar- ya weel?'—'A was better afoor A met thee'. Others have a distinctly North-Eastern besides Cumbrian flavour, such as 'Wheresta been till?' (*till* (to) is found in County Durham, and in Old Norse as *til*). 'Hoo is't, marrer?' (How are you, mate?), though Tyneside, is also typical of the West Cumbrian mining area.

For sentence-filling, Cumbria uses its full quota of *ers* and *ums* (as distinct from Scottish *ayms*). When rebuked about this habit, those who rely on them—does that include you?—reply that at least they know the right word and are just searching for it, whereas those who interlard their speech with *you know* and *you see* betray their ignorance and boorishness by making their listeners search for the word instead of giving it to them. The older Cumbrian relies much less on the unattractive *you know, See?, Right?, Do you get me?* and much more on *Seesta?,* which is used in conversation to focus attention, and is brought in so naturally that it induces a feeling of earnestness and friendliness.

Farewells adopt a fairly common pattern - 'Seea lang' (So long), 'A'll sithee', etc. The only one meriting a special remark here is 'Good neet!', which can be applied shortly after tea whilst it is still light, since Cumbria's *neet* has to do the work of both 'night' and 'evening'.

TIMES AND DIRECTIONS

These too deserve a word. Times include *foreneean* (morning) (now rare), *afterneean,* and *neet* as in *t'neet afoor* (the previous evening/night). For directions, people obey rough geography. For example from Kendal they go *up to Ammlesat* (Ambleside) and *down to Lancaster*. Years ago they would *gaan* (*go*) *up to Lunnon,* as if London were higher in altitude and a far superior place, though lower on the map; but now it is simply *to Lunnon,* indicating greater familiarity with travel and possibly Cumbria's increased status. What does stick out, though, is the reluctance of pronunciations and ideas to die. You may be asking your way in a village, where a smart lady appears at her bungalow to say, 'Manor Farm? You're nearly agin (next to) it'. Similarly it seems as if people are mentally consulting maps in their *scheealbooks* when they say 'E's fra Cummerland' or 'Ah lives i' Westmorland'.

WEATHER

The weather is a frequent source of conversation. A *burr roond t'meean* (ring round the moon) presages bad weather. It can be *muggy* (hot and damp), *bleeak* (bleak), *caald* (cold), *rowky* (raw), or *snerpy* (bitingly cold) when there is *rag* (hoar-frost) on the ground. You may have *thunner an' leetnin'* and a few *'ailstones* which (but only if you get wrapped up in the dialect) become *'ailsteeans.* The Lake District's rain is notorious, Seathwaite in Borrowdale with 125 inches a year being the wettest place in Britain; and when it rains heavily there it is said echoingly to come down *a reg'lar plosh.*

Cumbria also has some hated winds, the most feared being the Helm Wind, Cross Fell's own wind. It is often characterised by a thick bank of cloud resting along the Cross Fell range, probably caused by a cold wet wind blowing up the long eastern slopes and meeting warmer air from the west on the plateau. 'T'helm wind's on noo', locals will say, and when it roars down the Eden valley it is said to last for six weeks and make folk stay indoors. Its name comes from sailing-ship days, a good helm wind being excellent for making them scurry along. I am informed that the name was misinterpreted in the hearing of Archbishop Temple as 'all hell of a wind'!

Another infamous wind is that blowing from *Mosser Hooal,* an enormous hole near Cockermouth. Natives blame this rain-bearing wind on the hole. Less malicious is the *Borrowdale Sop* (note the term *soppin' wet*), which is a small single cloud floating around Sty Head Tarn. If it moves towards Langdale, rain is supposed to fall within the next twenty four hours, but if it moves into the Vale of St. John fine weather will continue. Millom natives take due warning if *Walney Pot,* that is the sound of seething waves, can be heard. Round the Kent estuary the same warning note used to be called the *sea call.* Of course there is much truth in such portents. My Windermere informants need no barometer, but accurately judge their weather by observing the sky and the lake, since almost all rain-bearing winds there come from the south-west. They say, 'If it's quite tidy (calm) doon there, thoo can wesh today.'

It is amusing to read what visitors have thought about Lakeland weather. Here are lines from *The Ambleside Weather Glass,* printed in *The Lakes Herald* of about the 1870s:

'When Wansfell wears a cap of cloud
The road of Brathay will be loud;
When mists come down on Loughrigg Fell,
A drenching day grayheads foretell...'

After proceeding like that it finishes ironically:

'When whales in Loughrigg Tarn they take,
When Robinson his boat shall sail
From Windermere to Patterdale,

...When no-one at the pier has cried
"This is the bus for Ambleside",
When all of us shall mend our ways,
The sun will shine for seven days!'

Its writer was Robinson, the optimistic sailor to which it alludes.

Cumbria's remarkable weather causes various intriguing sayings, such as:

'If it's fine, tak thi cooat;
If it's wet, please thisell'.

'When t'gadfly's aboot, t' weather's bad,' (farmers' saying).

'T' fells have gitten their shawls on' (of the first *snaa* (snow)).

'If t'wind's i't'Blue Gill (down Kirkstone), it'll rain'.

'Rain at flow, you may go to mow;
Rain at ebb, you may go to bed'. (Once chanted, despite its bad internal rhyme, in households round Morecambe Bay)

Finally here are two sayings about cloud wreaths on Cumbrian mountain summits portending despicable weather. Such sayings are quite common in Britain (others referring to Pendle Hill in Lancashire, Helsby Hill in Cheshire and Bredon Hill in Worcestershire): 'T'Owd Man (Coniston)'s gitten his cap on. It'll rain afoor t'day's out'.

And an ancient weather proverb:

'If Skidda wears a cap,
Scruffel (Criffel across the Solway) wots well o' that'.

This is another weak rhyme, meaning that bad weather on one side of the Solway is repeated on the other side. Nowadays people are apt to be very influenced by radio and television forecasts; consequently readers must judge for themselves which type of weather advice is more reliable.

PROVERBS AND OTHER SAYINGS

Much concentrated wisdom rests in Cumbria's proverbial sayings. Consider the business sense of 'Hire 'im with 'is britches' knees oot, nut 'is britches' arse' (that is, employ the hard worker). Here are more:

'She'd taak a banty cock into layan' an egg', (that is, she would talk the hind leg off a donkey)

'If we can't do thee a good turn, we waint do thee a bad 'un'.

'T'dooar sneck, that's where thoo gits sneck possit in cooartin' days', (when the door is snapped shut against the ardent lover)

A different type of axiom is:

'Nivver wed a scheealteacher or a nurse, they're nut ower mitch (nothing special)'. Luckily this advice is often very wrong.

Actual comparisons are generally unremarkable except for pronunciation of individual words, for example 'as black as neet', 'as daft as a brush' (because it cannot think or do anything itself), 'as strang as an ox', 'as leet as a fedder'. A more individual one is 'sturdit as a steg' (stupid as a gander).

There also exist a number of sayings specially prepared to trap the stranger, like 'Ast ivver seen a cuddy lowp a five-barred yat?'. To the initiated a translation is child's play - 'Have you ever seen a donkey jump a five-barred gate?'. However, a good deal of broad Cumbrian is utterly bewildering to the *off-comer*. At *Gersma Spooarts* (Grasmere Sports) an American and his wife overheard this conversation: 'Ah ken t'day when Jack felt (felled) Jim'.

'Duster? 'Oo lang sen?'

The Americans went away muttering that two Chinese were there.

CUSTOMS

Local customs usually give rise to special words. *Pace-eggin'* would take place. for example in Penrith and Furness, with children rolling their eggs to represent the stone rolling away to open Christ's tomb. Until at least about 1960 *laitin'* was still practised, for example in Matterdale, though on a reduced scale. For this a number of immediate neighbours went as a duty to prepare the corpse for burial and keep guard round it. When all was ready, there came the *biddin',* the personal invitation to the funeral. *Biddin'* to funerals took place up to the last war. The bidder would knock at every house in the village, saying something on the lines, 'You are requested to attend so-and-so's funeral tomorrow; lift at 11.30 a.m.' The introduction of the hearse has stopped this polite custom, but one of my informants, an *undertakker* himself, reminds me that even with modern facilities mourners can never be rushed.

Then there is *Tradesman's Holada,* sometimes called *t'Blackpool trip* since that resort is the most frequent destination. For the annual holiday corresponding to the *wakes* of South Lancashire and the West Riding, the nearest local term is *fair,* as with Egremont Crab Fair, held on a Saturday in late September. The *crab* part of that title comes from the scramble when several hundredweights of crab apples are thrown from a cart as it trundles down Egremont's Main Street.

Of more desperate and horrible customs, there was a rough cure for *the teeathwark* 'toothache' as applied to one of my helpers when he was a boy. At the blacksmith's he was told, 'Sit thisell o' theer, sit on t'stiddy (anvil). Git od (hold) o' that (*That* was the sharp end of the anvil). Od thi eead up ....', and out eventually came his tooth. The National Health Service has its advantages. Going farther into history, it is recorded that in 1832 a certain Joseph Thomson of Carlisle put up his wife for sale, advertising her most frankly as a 'torment, a domestic curse, a night invasion and a daily devil'. He added, 'She cannot make rum, gin or whisky, but she is a good judge of the quality from long experience'. After a 'Dutch auction' starting at 50 shillings he finally clinched the deal for one pound and a dog. What language, Cumbrian or otherwise, his *missus* used during this transaction is not stated.

GAMES

Apart from such standard games as soccer, cricket, *Union* and its more modern version of *League* as undergone in the *clarty* (sticky) mêlées of *Wukki'n, Whitehebben* and *Barrer,* there are more local activities, most famous of which is Cumberland and Westmorland wrestling, practised for example at *Gersma Spooarts* (Grasmere Sports Day). This has its special terminology including the *hype*, where you push your knee between your opponent's legs and lift him off the ground, and its refinement the *swing hype*, where you actually swing the poor fellow round once or twice. The *back heel* is useful. The *hank* looks dangerous, with the attacker twining his left leg round his opponent's right. For the *cross buttock* you put your buttock quickly under your rival's stomach, use it as a fulcrum and throw him over your head or shoulder. It is spectacular, but if it fails you are very apt to be thrown yourself, which can be painful. Of one thing you can be sure. This is genuine wrestling, with none of the showman's tricks of the *grunters an' groaners* in many seaside wrestling halls, like apparently plucking the hairs out of a man's chest one by one or stamping on his hands, which the ladies especially find so horrifying but which are so often simulated and pre-arranged.

It is recorded that some seventy years ago the men of Endmoor, Gatebeck, Hutton Roof and Lupton played *knurr and spell*. Men made their own sticks, *pum-heeds* (heavy ends of the bats) and even balls out of *hollin* (holly)-wood. Some players could knock the balls hundreds of yards. Balls were set on springs, which the batter tapped with his *pum-heed*. Up went the ball, but, if he missed catching it as it came down, he was out.

We could continue with more modern adult sports such as *pigeonin'*, ferreting and the like, but it would probably be more helpful now to turn to children's games for here some picturesque dialect survives. It is noticeable that amongst the most reliable features of the Scottish Linguistic Atlas are children's words, doubtless because teachers had the confidence of the children they listened to and knew their backgrounds. Thus children's games repay careful study and indeed those from Lakeland's *bairns* will not disappoint you.

'Itchy-pot (hopscotch) was a very expressive name since that is what you did—with your feet you hitched a piece of tile (hence the name *pot*), stone or anything handy. Children's hoops, called

boolers (as at Windermere) or with the diminutive ending *boolies* (as at Millom) were great playthings. The best were made of *thin iron* (*iron* being sounded with an *r*). As Norman Nicholson states, they were far better than those driven by blows of a stick. The hook, the sort the grocer uses to hang up bacon, was slipped under the curve of the *booley*, so that when you ran it ran beside you, as he aptly describes it, like a well-trained dog. It emitted a happy ringing sound, though you had to be careful to pull it back to keep pace with it down a steep hill. Many is the mile that I too have run as a boy to its sound, and many readers will surely remember them.

Bawlies were marbles bowled into a hole. "Ave y'any bawlies?' was a familiar cry, like the general exciting invitation 'Ar yer comin' oot to *laik* (play)?'. Leisure time often gave rise to pranks. A local baker recounts that as a youthful organ-blower he squirted *watter* from behind his curtain onto the head of the choirmaster, who next Sunday asked whether the church roof had been repaired. Yet in standard or private games, series contests or laughable pranks, what a world of memories is conjured up by thinking of the times when 'aal t'bairns is laikin' oot'!

SO MANY WORDS

Mrs Elizabeth Wright, wife of Joseph Wright, compiler of the great 1904 *English Dialect Dictionary,* states[1] that his work registered 'approximately 1,350 words meaning to give a person a thrashing...1,300 ways of telling a person he is a fool... and about 1,050 terms for a slattern'. It ignores descriptions applicable to kindly acts, wise men or efficient housewives apparently because they are more the norm, and normality does not excite comment.

It is therefore no surprise to find that Cumbrian dialects have a seemingly excessive number of words for striking and beating. Dickinson collected almost a hundred in his Cumberland glossary. You may blame it on pugnacious Viking ancestors or on rough unsettled conditions of the Border counties, but more likely it is just that extreme behaviour of any kind is well remembered. So we hear Cumbrians say, 'Thoo'll git a back-'ander', (and here this does not mean a bribe), 'Ah'll bash thi', 'Ah'll give 'im an 'ammerin'', 'Ah'll wallop/bat/cloot 'em' or 'Ah should be skelped for that'. In laughable sayings we find, for example, 'Ah'll clobber thee yan wid a wet fluke' or, in highly metaphorical terms, 'Tak this knuckle sandwich'. Similarly we hear 'Thoo's daft/gaumless', 'Thoo's a gowk (fool)', and in Barrow 'She's a right slag (slut)'. Yet average Cumbrian behaviour cannot be so different from that of normal people in other counties. The comfort is that a mere word-count

1. **Rustic Speech and Folk Lore,** Oxford, 1913.

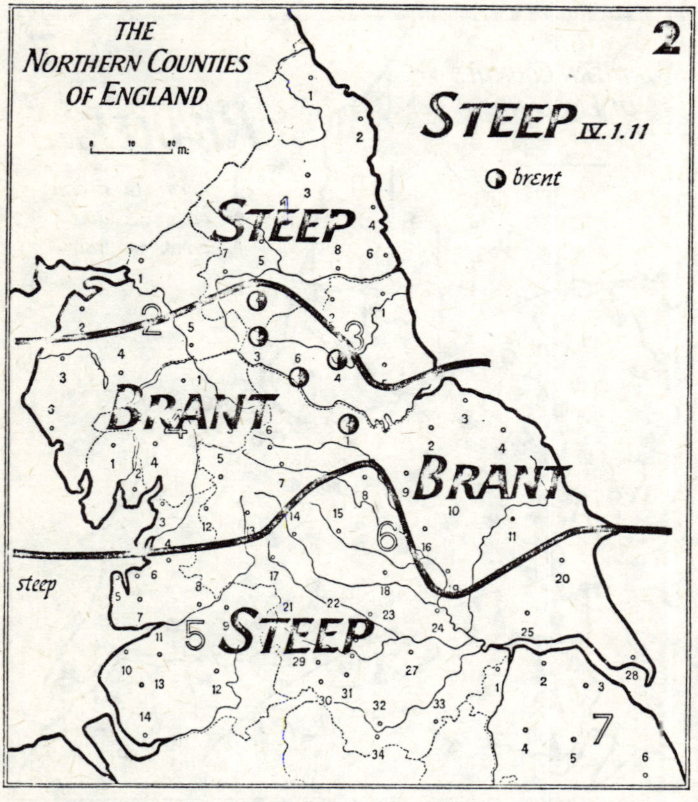

Geographical distribution of the dialect word 'brant', meaning 'steep'. (Map reproduced from 'Anglia', 1965).

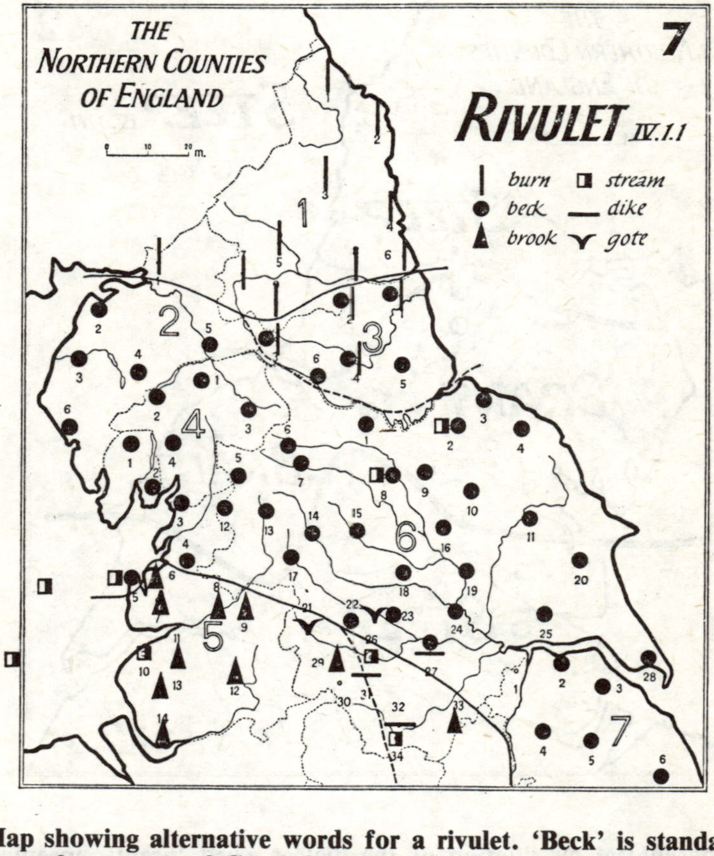

Map showing alternative words for a rivulet. 'Beck' is standard throughout most of Cumbria, except in the north-east where the Northumberland 'burn' is the norm. (Reproduced from 'Anglia', 1965).

gives a false picture: in dialect, as in so many other aspects of life, things are not always what at first they seem.

HOUSEHOLD WORDS

A house may be approached by a *lile ginnel* (little passageway). At the door, beside the door *jawms,* you ring the bell, knock or *oppen t'dooar sneck* (*sneck* applied originally to a wooden latch on a barn door). Inside is *t'parlour*, unless it is a bigger and better one, called *drawin'-room*, or (slightly more modern) *sittin'-room* or *front room*, or if its occupants have modernised their language the *lounge*. Now the old word *parlour* has taken a new lease of life in *milking-parlour*, a polished word for the cow-house.

The kitchen may have a *coppy* (stool) on which *t'bairns* will stand for mother to do their hair, *dishclouts, flooarclouts,* and certainly a *gully* (bread-knife). The *closet* became the *lav* and is now the *loo*. Above the bedrooms through a *man-'ooal* you enter the *cock-loft*, named from the times when it served as the arena for fighting-cocks.

Unfortunately many of the household words are disappearing along with the objects they stood for. The *weshas* (wash-house) has given way to spin-driers etc., so that the lady of the house no longer says, 'Ah mun (must) wesh t'towels today whativver. Ah'll gang an leet (light) t'fire under t'set-pot.' Round the *chimla* used to be the *tidy Betty*, fender, bellows (rarely *bellowses*) and *coorak* (coal-rake), which was 'a hafe-moon thing wid a hannel on'. Beds were heated not by electric blanket or even *het-watter bottle,* but by *warmin' t'oven-plate* and wrapping it in a blanket.

Outside will be the dustbin with all its *ket* or *kelter* (rubbish); and another type of *gully,* the grating for a drain. Farmers up Langdale way still use the *peatas* (peat-house), equal to the more modern *cooalas* (coal-house). In short, the Cumbrian dwelling like its occupants nurtures much dialect.

FOOD

The house topic leads naturally to food, which Cumbria can supply in abundance, although poorer folk used to subsist on an inadequate diet, being unable to afford butter and having 'meeat yance a week, Sunda'.

There is *Allonby toffee; Cumberland ceeak,* made with candied lemon peel, marmalade, raisins etc., *Gersma* (Grasmere) *shortceeak; Kendal mint-cake,* advertised as having been carried by Hillary and Tensing to the summit of Everest: and *rum butter*, which was originally a christening dish for visitors coming to see a new baby. *Tea-ceeak* in these parts means the sweet kind with currants, as opposed to *plain tee-ceeak*, differing therefore from parts of Britain which call it *currant tea-cake*. *Bannocks* come from the end of a mixing, when there is not enough flour to make a loaf. *Poddish*, stirred with a *thivel* (wooden porridge-stick), is made from *havermeal,* called by the very old timers *haver-bread,* and is referred to occasionally in the Scottish fashion as *them*, that is they think of the separate grains. *Plate-cakes* (tarts) such as Carlisle's *blackcurrant plate-cakes* also deserve special mention.

Other succulent dishes include *tayty-pot*, a stew with best neck of mutton; *black puddin'*, not just a Lancashire delicacy; and *yerb-puddin'*, still eaten and enjoyed round Penrith, for instance. It is made from a few young well-scalded nettles, a *pissybed* (dandelion) leaf or two, a handful of *dockins* (docks) and barley with seasoning. A Furness name for it is *Easterledge puddin'* because docks there were called *sour docks* or *easterledges*. Today it is easier to take an ice cream out of the fridge or use a *bought ceeak* (shop cake) than to gather all the *yerbs* to make the pudding. Then there was *jackat tayty* for supper, *sugar-shags* (bread slices spread with sugar) and other delicacies. What delights for the gourmet!

PARTS OF THE BODY AND CLOTHING

Since people are so interested in their bodies and rely on them so much, it is not remarkable that this topic stimulates many dialect words. Cumbrians have *lugs* instead of ears. Some are *lish* (active), others lazy, others are metaphorically *deed* (dead). They may have *anger-nails* (loose pieces of skin at the bottoms of finger-nails). If their toes turn in they are called almost unanimously *pigeon-toed*; those with the opposite deformity are *splaa-footed* or, according to teenagers, have *kipper feet*. *Kag(gy)-handed* people are more common now that left-handedness is not punished at school, but there still seems a reluctance to accept the non-conformer. That is probably why Barrovians, for instance, call Roman Catholics *left-leggers* or *left-footers* as if they behave and accomplish things in an awkward way, even though Vickers, the famous Barrow family firm, was Catholic.

Clothing too gives rise to local words, from the *muffler* (neckerchief) to the *tin tab* (tag) on a bootlace. Up to the Great War, boys had jackets, *ganseys*, and *knee-britches* because these were cheapest and lasted longer; and they wore clogs. Girls had the same footwear, with iron heels and long black stockings. Their clogs were shaped like shoes and no trouble to walk good distances in. A rarer clothing word appeared recently when a Furness farmer excused himself, saying he had left his *kytle i't'field*, his *kytle* being a short working-coat. The body and its garments have thrown up an array of special terms.

ANIMALS

Here again a formidable list of unusual names trips from Cumbrian tongues. To cite just a few, in birds we have *yowlet* for a grown owl besides a young one, *scobby* (chaffinch), *dunnock* (hedge-sparrow), *sea-parrots* (puffins) at St. Bees Head, *watter-ousels* (dippers – seen on the River Mint, Kendal), not forgetting the *gowk* (cuckoo), used also in terms of rebuke like *'Thoo gert gowk!'* (You great idiot!). Other Cumbrian bird-names are carefully shown in an excellent article by K.G. Spencer in *Journal* No. 14 (1965) of *The Lancashire Dialect Society*. They include from the Duddon Valley *Jimmy Crane* (heron), *fellfold* (fieldfare) and *spink* (chaffinch); from Walney Island *seapie(t)* (oyster-catcher); from Flooksburgh *dykie* (hedge-sparrow), *grey duck* (wigeon), *pied duck* (shelduck), and *sea-mouse* and *mouse-bird* (dunlin). Helena Oliphant has an instructive bird-name article in The Lakeland Dialect Society's *Journal* no. 36 (1974), which mentions among many others the *watter nanny* (sedge warbler), *Bessy dooker* (dipper), *storm cock* and *fell throssel* and *shreely* (mistle-thrush), *screape* and *hedder-bleat* (snipe), *blackie* or *merle* (blackbird), *whaup* (curlew) and *doggenel* (eagle). She finishes with the curious complaint, 'Waat for, Ah wonder, have weh nea dialect neame for t'robin reed breest?'

Insects include the *pissimer* (ant); and the *gadbee*, which strikes sheep and stings cows' legs so that they gad about. Another animal was the *foomart* (polecat), meaning 'foul marten' because of its odour, though it is probably now extinct in Lakeland. There are also *rattens* (rats), *kitlins* (kittens) and *cuddies* (donkeys), along with *mowdies* (moles). In fact, one of my language helpers is a most experienced *mowdy-catcher*, and much appreciated as the land round his farm is *plagued wi' mowdies*.

Tourists may be astonished at the local ways of attracting animals. To pigs, the Cumbrian shouts 'Giss, giss!' – pigs, farmers remind me, are not all stupid, and indeed 'Owt (anything) can be trained to come'. To cows they call 'Cush, cush!' or 'Howp, howp!', to hens 'Chuck, chuck!' and to ducks rather mundanely 'Come, come!'. For horses they may just rattle a bucket; but horses, at least the old ones, certainly understood Cumbrian language in responding to *Gee up!*, *Haa!* (Go right), *Gee back!* (Go left), *Come ower!*, or even *'Step ower t'top o't'stitch* (ridge)'.

Amongst animals it is impossible to forget sheep, especially in Cumbria. There are *yows* (ewes), and *tups* (rams), and (clearly abbreviations) *twinters* (two year olds) and *trinters* (three year olds). They may be marked with *red rud*, and be *liggin'* (lying) on the grass or *lowpin'* (leaping) about. *Heaf-gannin'* sheep are named from their *heaf*, their own limited area, which seems yet another Norse word, probably from Icelandic *hefd* (habitual place). Sheep suffer from diseases. If they eat tormentil, they become *souted* and soon deteriorate, though removal to good pasture can cure them in two to three weeks. Worse is for a sheep to be attacked by maggots, making the farmer moan, 'Wicks 'ave gitten at it, it's wickt.'

Finally the subject of sheep cannot be left without mentioning the old sheep-scoring numerals, where you counted up to twenty and then re-started. It must be stressed, however, that except among children or for the benefit of impressing credulous tourists this old Gaelic method of sheep-counting disappeared from Lakeland probably late last century. A couple of examples will suffice:

(from Borrowdale) yan, tyan, tethera, methera, pimp (5), sethera, lethera, hovera, dovera, dick (10), yan-a-dick, tyan-a-dick, tether-a-dick, mether-a-dick, bumfit (15), yan-a-bumfit, etc. up to giggot (20).

(from Seathwaite) aina, peina, para, peddera, pimp, ithy, mithy, owera, lowera, dig (10), ain-a-dig, pein-a-dig, etc.

No wonder the old farmers eventually found a better way of counting aloud than with confusing runs of similar sounds like *tethera, methera...sethera, lethera*, especially as our two sample counts have only *pimp* (note the Welsh *pump*) in common. There really are benefits in 'modern maths'. This apart, Cumbria's general and rural dialect maintains an impressive store of individual local words.

5. How They Talk in Carlisle

THIS is an effort to bring Cumbrian language more into modern focus by examining the speech of its city and administrative centre, Carlisle. Although Cumbrian towns and villages are singularly lucky in retaining so well many aspects of their traditional vernacular, Carlisle should never be forgotten. After all, it shelters about 100,000 people, which is more than one Cumbrian in five.

A diligent search of all issues of The Lakeland Dialect Society *Journal* has unearthed only one direct reference to Carlisle speech. It is a short interesting poem with a sting in its tail, but, although it was written by a Carlisle grammar schoolboy, one hesitates to assume that it is in a Carlisle, or *the* Carlisle, dialect. Nevertheless its *lonnin'* for 'lane,' *ya* for 'one' and *nut* for 'not' are certainly true of the city; and, perhaps especially as an antidote to the technical discussion which follows, the poem seems well worth repeating here:

'A Chance Meeting' by John Trunnion

Es Ah wus gan down't loonin' ya day
Ah met me a lass in a reet fine array,
"Whee ista gannan when thee's lukin se well?"
"Just min' thee own business for Ah's nut ganna tell."
"Nay, Cum on lass, divent be shy
Tha'll tell m'all or Ah'll nut let thee by."
"Ah's gan te git wedded," she sed wid a grin,
"Se git oot et road or tha'll mebbe meet 'im."

As a short pithy poem it is most attractive but for a learned dissection of living Carlisle speech we need some wider base. One difficulty is, of course, that citizens anywhere do not normally go about reciting poetry.

Little help comes either from Army memories. My first contacts with Carlisle are from 1942, when, as a Lancastrian, I was somewhat unwillingly drafted into the care of the Border Regiment for recruit training at Bitts Park (curious name—apparently a corruption of Butts). Memories of those days are still vivid—of us straggling 'ex-civvies,' completely out of step, attempting to march up Castle Street to our new quarters; of very successful lessons in camouflage but peculiar ones on the Brough firing range where, forced to fire without glasses in a gas mask, I could not see and shot for safety rather into the air and to the instructor's panic. (Worse still, on a previous week another recruit had shot over the butts and killed a cow on the Solway Marches beyond.)

These conditions have gone and their language with them. A busy road now runs south of Carlisle Castle and Bitts Park at its foot is military no more. Apart from on visits like one to a *flicks* in East Carlisle where the admission charge for the hard back benches was *thrippens,* others to educated friends, and to *t'Sally Army,* where we had literally to sing for our suppers (good ones, though), the Carlisle language met in the 1940s was chiefly from some instructors and typically Army—extraordinarily vivid but irrelevant to this article.

An indirect method of considering Carlisle speech would be to scrutinise the 1889 results collected by A.J. Ellis from Dalton, only four miles South South West of the city centre. Much of this, when at last decoded, seems very accurate. He has, for instance, *jon lonin* for 'that lane', *beern* for 'child', and a diphthong *Ei,* standing for a pronunciation *ey,* in 'like, mine and times', which corresponds to present-day usage. Yet he includes doubtful matters and at least one error. He has *jens* for 'once'—compare Carlisle *jance;* and *mek,* a more southerly form of 'make'—compare current Carlisle *mak,* plus *mek.*

Another possible way of finding clues to Carlisle speech would be to analyse the impressive results of the Leeds University *Survey of English Dialects* from places closest to the city. The nearest was Longtown, eight miles north. Here, however, the trouble is not the undoubted accuracy of the results but the fact that they came by the principles of that survey from a totally different kind of community, a small farming one. It is not reasonable to expect the average Carlislian to know specialised farming terms, for example, a female sheep between first and second shearings or a T-shaped plough-beam end.

More than this: many general terms gathered from Longtown are strange to Carlisle. They include Longtown's *ask* (newt), *duck-toed, kirk, jy, neave, rine* (hoar-frost), *threeap* (argue), *yince* (once) and *yist* for (respectively), Carlisle *asp* (mispronunciation?), *pigeon-toed, churrach* plus *chuch, askew, fist, rime, fratch, yance* and *yeast.* Other Cumbrian words which now seem dead in the city, if indeed they ever appeared there, include *April gowk* (April fool), *giversome* (hungry), *sitfast* (core) of boil, *sotter* (boil slowly) and *swammel* (to scramble, climb).

My authority for the comparisons with present-day Carlisle is the result of enquiries and conversations with many people who all deserve warm and sincere thanks. A vital helper was Jack Elliott, aged seventy-six, ex-train driver of 55, Broad Street, a very natural and fluent Carlisle speaker who acted as anchor-man by guiding me most patiently round the city to meet his many friends and acquaintances—up a *ginnel,* past the tithe barn, *doon a clarty loonan,* round the market and all over. There were also William Fraser, aged seventy eight, Joseph Stalker, aged seventy-nine and other members of the Carlisle Veterans' Association, one of whose December 1976 meetings I had the honour of attending.

I was also enabled to analyse from tape the speech of participants at a Cummerland Neet Association dinner and annual meeting. For this I was greatly indebted to Harold Forsyth and members of the Association which, revived in 1954, shared many of the Lakeland Dialect Society's aims in working to 'keep alive a love of Cumberland, its customs, dialect and music', and has appropriately merged with our own Society. The *Cummerland Neeters,* like the rest of our Society and other dialect societies, live in the present and are not seeking to popularise a dead thing like a fossil in a museum. At a recent *Cummerland Neet,* held at Dalston, Tim Pitt of Radio Carlisle was the principal speaker. Very useful help for my searches also came from Mrs. Elliott; Mr H.W. Hodgson, librarian at Tullie House; Miss Nan Dawson and Radio Carlisle, who at one point interviewed me from a phone box in distant Cheshire.

First contact with Carlisle for the purpose of this analysis was surprisingly odd: a long distance telephone conversation with a Carlislian who had lost her voice. However, when her husband was brought to the phone, speech became clearly and decisively local. To my early inquiries about whether to bring a tape-recorder, the advice given was that it was better still just to listen—*'ing about roond t'market an' tak thi chance.* This was the type of procedure adopted.

From the details already given it must be clear that the Carlisle talk concentrated upon was that of the older generation. This important but limited approach was chosen for three reasons. Firstly only a short time was at my disposal, Carlisle being merely one of many urban dialects being investigated. Secondly it is a sad fact that such speech may be less easily available in a few more years. Thirdly a basis must be established against which to compare the changing speech of younger generations. This survey ought to be only a start, which will perhaps encourage others to extend it especially by inquiring into the language of Carlisle's youngsters.

Carlisle talk is particulary interesting for having so many local words and pronunciations. They hit you whenever you meet a true Carlislian—if that is the right word for a dweller in what is called, historically and without thought of Christmas, *Carrel.* 'Noo then', he may say, 'Ah's gay—a thrang (very busy) an' a've 'ad a sair darrick (great difficulty) wi' yon job, but Ah'll di-oo a wun for yer bi't'fo'teenth'.

Some terms are amazingly different from Standard English. At the *smiddy* (blacksmith's shop) you may lift the *snick* (door-latch) and see inside a *stee* (ladder). Dandelions are *pissymothers*, minnows are *liggies* and the bigger ones *cock liggies*. Other animals include *the paddock, jinny spinner, mowdiwarp* and *urchin*, respectively for the frog, daddy-longlegs, mole and hedgehog. People can be *lish* (active), *cravakt* (stiff) or *gowk-anded* (clumsy). They may suffer from *keens* or *hacks* (split skin on the hands) or wrench an *oxter* (armpit). Their hair may be *cawf-licked*. Like roads they may be *slape* (slippery) (for example ''E's a slape feller.'), and *haffle* (hesitate) and *maffle* (bluster). If, on the other hand, one of them is a fool, you would be wise not to *fratch* (argue) with him but to *flaatch 'im* (wheedle him).

Some of the proberbial sayings sound unusual. For instance, when banns have been called, Carlisle church-goers will say, 'Ther 'ingins are in t' bell-rayaps', literally 'Their hangings are in the bell-ropes'. In ordinary numerals and measurements too, one may find along with fairly normal pronunciations like *seven* and *ten* other queer-sounding ones like *yaa fyut* (one foot). Nor are such terms mere curiosities: they fly about, though chiefly from the lips of the elderly, *t' mayan o' t' day-a* (most of the day).

In comparing Carlisle dialect with those of other regions, it is no surprise to find many affinities with nearby Durham and Northumberland. Prominent are *intil* (into) and *til* (to) as in *'e rit til 'am* (he wrote to him); *byre* for the old fashioned cow-house; *cuddy* for a donkey (ultimately from St. Cuthbert); *lile* and *leyl* for little; and *bit* for (bit of), for example in *'as a bit chat*. Also reminiscent of the North East, for example of Newcastle, is a very high sound approaching short *ee* as in *'e's week* (*-wick*, lively). Carlisle terms well-known too in North Yorkshire include *addle* (to earn), *fettle* (-mend) *t' feyer, leh-ak* (to play) and *fra* (from) as in *fra yan*. Other very northern features include *oo* from Old English *u* as in *aboot* (about), *ang* as in *lang* (long) and *steg* (gander) a word previously heard also in the North Midlands but which has been retreating northwards. What did seem surprising was to find traces of speech with an apparently South Western ring; as *'twas gawn* (it was gone), *'twas snawed up, as 'tis* (as it is). A contributory factor might be the demands of rapid conversation.

As expected, Scandinavian words abound. Moors are *fells*; dirty children are *clarty* or *mucky*; and, if you are listening inattentively, you may well receive the rebuke, 'Git thi lugs cleaned oot, oppen thi lugs,' with the Viking-borne *lug* for 'ear'.

Even the oldest generation does not cling obstinately to every dialect word in its repertoire. *Parlish* as in 'There's parlish (very) few folk,' is still known but has died from ordinary usage. The favourite intensifier with older people is *gay*. You will hear, 'That's a gay lish (very active) coo,' or 'She's a gay poor soul.' There's a *gay* lot of it about, and quite unconnected with the modern meaning of 'homosexual'.

The language, then, sounds quite Northern although it appears at different levels of broadness. For example, of words descending from those containing Old English *á*, we find rising diphthongs in *tyal* and *tyel* (tale) and *yam* (as in 'Ah's gaan yam'); *eea* in *bleead* (blade) and *seeam* (same), and a falling diphthong *ay-a* modified by Received Pronunciation in for example *clayas* (clothes) and *gayat* (gate)—*yat* for the latter belongs outside the city in Cumbria.

Modern conditions are pretty baffling, and thus it is all the more important to separate the vernacular of Carlisle from that of its hinterland. At Kirkbampton, for instance, the wonderful local dialect is subject to outside influences—for example, those of retired farmers from different parts of the county. In Carlisle itself, the strongest Northern elements are being diluted. They are, it is claimed, being kept alive on special occasions and by the conversation of the elderly. Pessimists grieve that traditional dialect is quickly dying and is 'lost in a city'. Yet this is much more unlikely with Carlisle speech, rapidly though it does fluctuate. In my view it will, for the foreseeable future, retain many special characteristics. So it should, for it would be soul-destroying if we all could and had to speak perfect Standard English or even a standard never-changing Cumbrian.

Some Carlisle speakers may be at a disadvantage on formal occasions. In his prayers I heard a lay preacher consoling *hill 'ealth;* whilst in stressing words like *turn* his usual flapped *r* became a strongly rolled one, turning into something like *turran*, which to a stranger would seem to distract from the important thing, his message. However, such irregularities were either unnoticed or were rightly being ignored by the rest of the congregation.

We must take care not to confuse local with social dialect. The desirable area of Stanwix is at one extreme, whilst people are supposed to 'speak rougher' in the new council estates of Botcherby, Harraby and Raffles, where there is more violence. This seems largely a social difference. Another stems from the efforts of many city folk to talk more refined. 'My wife speaks very broken glass,' complained one informant; though his wife, with her allegedly 'cut-glass' voice, replied that he persisted in his dialect out of obstinacy. But it is a fact, in Carlisle as elsewhere, that men as a rule tend to speak more broadly than the ladies, probably because the latter worry more about how dialect might limit their children's careers. However, even Carlisle housewives may be unintelligible to a stranger when they talk, for example of reasty bacon being *waffy*, or of *wussed stockins*, or of leaving the kettle *slutherin'* (simmering) *on t'feyer.*

There has been a strong Scottish influx of population, especially from Glasgow, because of the railway. Carlisle Station may now look more deserted after Lord Beeching's ruthless surgery of its local lines, but the city has for long been an important railway centre. Like most people, Carlislians are slightly suspicious of all *off-comers,* whom they describe as 'Them's the folk at's come in', but they have a special wariness and sometimes open hatred of the Scots. As it is so much a border stronghold, the last English bastion before the Scottish frontier and one that has had to accept the invasion of Scottish armies, it is not surprising that parts of Carlisle harbour intense national rivalries. The recent upsurge of Scottish Nationalism may be adding to this frustration of some Carlislians at having to put up with settlers from what seems an increasingly alien country. This dislike extends to Glasgow dialect, for they say of it, 'Calisle's bad but Glasga's 'orrible.'

Place-names evidence some resistance to invasion by the Scottish language. Just as in the North East *burn* is unable to encroach over the Tyne-Tees watershed, streams flowing south into the Tees being *becks,* so in Cumbria *burn* is regular at Longtown eight miles north of the city, but the Carlisle word is *beck.* However, other Carlisle terms remind us strongly of Scottish. They include *canny,* as in *canny awld Cummerland; sark* for a shirt; *bairns*; and of course *ken,* famous in 'D'ye Ken John Peel?'

Carlisle pronunciation, perhaps even more than its words, reminds one of Scotland. Like country Scottish it sounds very clear and precise. Most remarkable is the guttural *gh,* which in England is practically extinct. Nevertheless it must once have been a very familiar sound, for it is established in the spelling of quite a number of common words such as *right, night, straight.* In Carlisle I have heard it most often finally after a back vowel as in *bagh,* for 'back', *Jogh* for 'Jock', and *lugh!* for 'look!'. Mr. Elliot pointed across the lines of Carlisle Station to talk about the *blogh* for the block of buildings including the refreshment room on the platform opposite. Another Carlisle veteran gratefully accepted a lozenge, saying *It's slochenin'* (It's slaking) that is 'It relieves the throat'. These examples should be compared with the statement made in 1889 by A.J. Ellis for 'Edenside', his area D31 in which he included Carlisle: '(kwh) labial guttural. German auch; Scotch loch. Now nearly obsolete.' In 1976 it was certainly still alive.

It seems that either Carlisle's guttural is a fairly recent importation from Scotland, as the city lies on the extreme north of Ellis's 'Edenside' area; or that Carlisle has preserved an ancient dialect feature which the surrounding countryside has not, which would be unusual for any British city; or else that the sound was more frequent in 'Edenside' in Ellis's time than he believed, and so its death is taking longer. Present evidence favours the last theory.

Carlisle's *r* is very frequently flapped and sometimes rolled. Like the Scottish rolled *r* it greatly distorts words. For example, a stranger hearing *'e fair gurrned,* even if he sensed that *fair* was just an intensifier meaning 'very much', might imagine *gurrned* to be a local word of wildly exotic meaning, whereas it simply means 'grinned'. What makes such a word puzzling is not only the metathesis of *r* (that is *r* changing places with its preceding vowel) but also the nature of Carlisle's *r* itself, with the tongue moving so much that you tend to remember the *r* more than the vowel it introduces.

The man-in-the-Carlisle-street can make other comparisons with present-day Scottish. An *aw* sound, long or half-long, sometimes replaces short *o*, as in *Kid 'em awn,* 'Tease them'; and *gawb,* slang for 'mouth' as in *shut yer gawb!* Supporters of Carlisle United *leyk footbo'.* Notice here the light *l* starting *leyk* and *l's* absence after the back vowel in *footbo',* as occurs in Glasgow. On occasion the speech comes nearer still to Glasgow's, as when the fans at Brunton Park talk about *fïtbo',* with the short vowel between *i* and *u* so characteristic of many Scots.

Carlisle's grammar sounds original and certainly not what Richard Baker and other announcers prefer on the B.B.C.'s nine o'clock news. There are double negatives, as *dunt want nee tea* 'wants no tea'. The relative pronoun is usually *at* and occasionally *watt* (rhyming with *cat*) but sometimes omitted as from, 'There's three or four fellers comes (who come) in.' We meet *for to* (in order to), *or* (than) for example in *mair streyks or owt else* (more strikes than anything else), and often what seems a wholly unnecessary *a* in expressions like *git a wun* (get one). We find unorthodox past tenses such as *telt* (told), *spock* (spoke) and *coom* (came); and for emphasis a way of slipping in the demonstrative pronoun *that,* as for instance 'E's a canny leyl feller, that.' Sometimes, to add to the confusion, there arise words that are grammatically unneeded, *but 'ooivver* we'll try to ignore them.

Phonetically speaking, we have occasional *d* for voiced *th* as in *fadder* (father) and *wid 'em* (with them). Compare also *wid a grin* in our opening poem, some dental *t's* so that for example 'tractor' sounds like *thractor,* and as noted above some disappearing *l's* as from *pow-jumpan'* (pole jumping). Moreover, even speakers attempting received pronunciation may simplify difficult consonant clusters, so that for example, a secretary becomes a *seccatary.* Also, as already noted, many variations are possible in the phonetic layers. For instance 'night' may be pronounced, even by the same speaker, as *neet* (rarer) besides *neyt.*

The intonation also seems different. 'Carlisle is sing-song,' I was told. It does have that tendency, but much less so than other areas remote from the heart of England, such as Northumberland and Tyneside, Scotland, Ireland and the Welsh border counties. 'Carlislians,' I was further informed, 'cut their words and so talk faster.' Mechanical evidence does support the claim that Carlisle speech is more rapid, generally speaking, than what one hears in more rural Cumbria. I have, for example, a long tape from a Keswick area man speaking at about 102 words per minute, which may be compared with Harold Forsyth's enthralling tape of a *Cummerland neet* where the rate, excluding songs and laughter, was just over 172 words per minute, and that for formal speeches!

To prevent confusion, a few fine details need mentioning. If you encounter the threat, 'Ah'll skelp yer ass,' this does not imply that you possess a donkey. *Kept it* as in 'A ken a kept it,' can mean 'retained it' as in Standard English or else 'caught it.' When men converse for long, this pursuit seems to have higher status than when ladies resort to it. The men are just *crackin'* but their 'better halves' are *clattin'*; and you will meet the remark, though the lady concerned is very much alive, 'She's a turble body to clat (a renowned gossiper).' However, a member of either sex can be labelled angrily a *blatherskeyt*.

To illustrate Carlisle language in connected fashion, let us conclude with a snatch of Clara Fyfe's speech to the Cummerland Neet Association. She freely admitted that she had been brought up in Botchergate and never talked any other way. Hers is no isolated example of the vernacular, as any visit to a Lakeland Dialect Society meeting or conversation with an elderly native would well prove, but at least it gives the flavour:

'A once went an' stayed with a friend—a wasn't in very good 'ealth in them days—yer wadn't think it to look at us (me) noo —but in them days a wazzent an' a stopped at this faam'oos an' the servant girl, as tha called 'em then, she was a maasterpiece at it (i.e. dialect) an' a wasn't eatin' very weel an' she said to me one day, "Thoo kysty little—," she says, "Git at it!" an' a looked at 'er an' a said, "A caan't." Sha said, "A tell tha watt—thoo'll bi glad to get it thrawn at tha o'er a bawk afooar thoo guz oot o' the wurrald." Well, of course, I asked mey most (best) friend efter "Wat did she mean bi sayin' that?" "Aw," she said, "of course ya little blatherskeyt, ya wad lay yer lugs up for owt ya shouldn't 'ear..."'

For its novelty to the newcomer, its variety and its preservation of so much that is historical, Carlisle's dialect must surely rank as one of the most interesting city dialects in the British Isles. If you are unimpressed with it, then , as dwellers in *Carrel* might say, there's *summat wrang*; you're a *dummle-'eed, sackless, gormless* or *nicked i' t' eed*. And they would be right. So, whoever you are, never let them bring that charge. Whenever you have the good fortune to hear it, or when you yourself speak it, just rest content with the wealth and vigour of Carlisle's living dialect.

6. Cumbrian Humour

Cumbrians have the undeserved reputation of being humourless. It is supposed to be so hard to make them laugh. Perhaps this unfortunate reputation springs from the absence in Cumbria of a vast chain of workingmen's clubs on the Lancashire and Yorkshire pattern, or because Cumbria has nothing equivalent to Blackpool's 'Golden Mile' or the drolleries of Liverpudlians. More probably it comes because the county harbours many retired people, and it is considered that in the evening of life, trying to cope with the physical difficulties of advancing years, most elderly people want to enjoy peace and quiet, not to frolic with flippant youngsters. If little Alfie next door chasing his ball bursts through your fence and knocks down your runner beans, you do not guffaw with delight or attempt some sick joke like 'trey mi tayters next'—you feel like clobbering him.

As a retirement area Cumbria also has an excess of women, whereas humour is commonly thought to be chiefly the property of the man. When you want a store of it, you are told to see some local male, particularly a tradesman such as the local barber or cobbler. It seems to be forgotten that housewives and even headmistresses, having to cope so long with the odd behaviour and language of their children, cannot be divorced from humour. Women in this respect are not necessarily inferior. We should not support the Cumbrian who boasted, 'Aa's t'aadest (the oldest) in't'parish.' 'Nay, thoo's nut,' retorted his wife, naming one or two ladies. 'Oh, women,' he said disdainfully, 'Ah dinna tak coont (take count) o' them.' In fact, however, plenty of humour and from both sexes bubbles out in Cumbria.

Firstly, though, we should define humour. Let us exclude for the moment stray weird remarks from foreigners settled in the county, like that of the Greek lady during a dustbin strike who, when asked by kindly neighbours, 'Oo's thi dustbin?' replied, 'Very well.' These are mere language difficulties not peculiar to Cumbria. I would also dearly like to exclude many puns, such as 'Hey, mister! Nay, Ah've fun (found) her.' Local they may be, but they are too artificial. At the other extreme we should ignore witty remarks heard by chance in

Cumbria but actually quite unlocal, like the grumble that under the Tories man exploits man but under Labour it is vice versa. Let us stick to Cumbrian humour in its commonest forms.

Practical jokes have always been a favourite amusement of some people, and not, I am sorry to say, just schoolchildren. There is a variety of little green-and-pink apples called *Kendal Dollies,* said to have been grown specially by a Lyth valley man for his *missus* to make toffee apples to sell at local agricultural shows. They are early ripeners and eagerly sought by amateur gardeners because they are such prolific croppers. One enthusiast planted an apple tree and next morning was mystified to see it already bearing its *Kendal Dollies*; to hasten nature, his neighbour had slipped out in the hours of darkness and strung to it some appropriate fruit.

The forms that practical jokes take are legion. A favourite is for a group of Cumbrians in a pub to keep an *aad 'un* talking so that he misses his point. To work this mild amusement is quite easy. When the *aad-teymer* (old-timer) opens his tale with for example, 'Ah meind when we 'ad yon streyk doon t'pit,' you butt in to ask, 'Was that where they had the red-headed *gaffer* from South Wales?' This halts his story dead in its tracks while he deals with the irrelevant question. A pal surreptitiously times the whole process and he who drags out the longest story wins. A more out-of-the-way joke is recorded as having been played on a farmer in a Cumbrian hostelry by taking his pony out of his cart shafts and reharnessing it the wrong way round. When the farmer, now a little *sozzled,* emerged, he looked at his pony and mumbled, 'Aw, so thoo's kicked it ower thi head. Well, thoo can kick it back again.' A very modern joke, caused by fear of wildly escalating water charges, was started by a local *bobby* who, having obtained some official notepaper, sent his neighbour across the road an 'official' warning that too much water had been used and that henceforth the family was limited to seven daily flushes of the *loo.* After receiving this, the wife was very angry when her husband exceeded the total. The joke was so well appreciated, at least by the sender and his pals, that it caught on and appeared sporadically in Lancashire and Cheshire. So with jokes like those described, apple-pie beds, telephone hoaxes and all the rest, it is hard to deny a local though often misplaced sense of practical humour.

However, as elsewhere, by far the most frequent jokes are the idiot stories, like that of the Penrith-area farmer on his way to market who was asked by a friend living far from the station to see if there was a parcel there for him. Late that evening he was spotted returning and shouted to urgently about the parcel. 'Aye,' he yelled in reply, 'It's theer alright.' Of course some of the fool stories take a great deal of believing, like that of the old lady noticed standing on one leg as her train crept above the water in the Kent estuary, saying that she didn't want to put down any more weight than was necessary *gaain' o'er 'ere*.

Intriguingly certain areas have become notorious for harbouring fools, and in the Lake District this sorry reputation has descended most on Borrowdale. Correspondence in *Cumbria* for April, 1952, for instance, noted the man in Borrowdale who made a boat in his attic and could not get it out. Other Borrowdalesmen are supposed to have seen quicklime smoking and used water to extinguish the fire, to have mistaken a red deer for a horned horse, and—best known story of all—to have tried to wall in the *gowk* (cuckoo) in order to have perpetual spring. As the bird just cleared the high wall to escape, one dalesman said dejectedly, 'By gow! If we'd only put on another row o' steeans, we'd have hed it!' *Gowk* is also Cumbrian for a fool and thus, if the story is to be believed, the worst *gowks* of Borrowdale were not in truth birds but irrational dalesmen. Furthermore it was allegedly a Borrowdale man who went to Keswick market and had a convivial time. On his return home friends boarded up his windows. He woke next morning, thought he had overslept a day and it was night again, and went back to bed, so missing a day's work. When his senses had cleared, his friends laughed at him, 'Thoo aald fyool!' Correspondence in *Cumbria* magazine asks why such stories attach to particular places. Is it that the locals have a perverse pride in their daftness? Rather not, I think, because no-one likes to be thought truly mad. It must be a label given by outsiders who imagine themselves superior to the country bumpkin.

Tall stories fall into an intermediate class. You know the type. 'Tha (they) grew a marrer. It was that big it pushed t'garden wa' ower sooa me an' oor Bob tried to lift it an' wi couldn't, wi didn't knaa what to deea. Bob went for t'six-foot cross-cut saa an' we saad it i' two an' took it away twice i't'barrer.' Or there is the story of the farmer who lost a turkey, then another and then another till he said, 'Ah'll lose neea mair. Ah'll keep watch.' He dozed off and woke up trussed and ready for market. Here one wonders whether the fool is the listener supposedly taken in by the account or the narrator who expects it to be credible. Perhaps into the same class should go those sayings which, though foolish, betray a certain defensive obstinacy like, 'Missel fost, then t'missus, then me agin. Then Ah'll see what's left for thoo.'

In direct contrast to the village idiot jokes are those where the apparent idiot turns the tables. They may take the form of a protest, sometimes roughly worded. For example, a parson said to a Lakeland chain-smoker, 'If the Lord had intended you to smoke, He would have put a chimney on the top of your head,' to which his parishioner replied, 'And if He'd meant thoo to tak snuff, He'd a' put thi nooase t'other way up.' Another example comes from the farm. 'By God, Bob! These is lile (little) eggs?' 'If thoo thinks my lile hens is gaan to stretch their lile legs to lay big eggs for thee, thoo's mistacken.' A second way to turn the tables is gently to pull the stranger's leg. A Kendal-area farmer, asked by a youngster how many piglets his sow was going to have, replied with studied foolishness, 'Ee, lad, it mud a' (might have) a single 'un or it mud a' twins.' Another farmer, from Windermere, said to a shivering boy, 'Noo, thoo can come to this side o't'railins if thoo thinks it's any waarmer here.' Such sayings are quite witty but the hearers would not realise it, being only lads.

With a strong conviction of their cwn superiority comes the Cumbrian's preference for the *status quo* over new-fangled methods, possibly imported from other areas. The dalehead farmer said scornfully, 'We mak nowt o' eddication up here: we uses our brains instead.' Considering the difference between book intelligence and ordinary *gumption*, there may well be some truth in this. Of the same ilk was the action of the Cumbrian farmer who returned his pre-war cracked-windowed van to the garage. 'What's up, George?' 'Nut much, but it's nut rattlin' reet.' Or there is the story of his friend who protested, 'Ah's nut mucky, Ah change mi shirt yance a week,' and, when his questioner argued that he changed his every day, replied, 'Then thoo mun be a lot muckier nor me.' Again there was grandad's answer to his grandson's query about why he did not buy a better T.V. set 'Nay, lad, I'se too aald for change. I'se only just getten used to t'folks in this yan.' Such a belief in the worth of native customs appears at its strangest in matters of etiquette. 'Have a nice drink of tea, grannie,' said a considerate girl, 'Ah've already saucered an' blowed it.'

Old buildings besides old customs cause what to the stranger, in sharp contrast to the native, are jokes. In some areas the farm toilet was over the pigsty, approached by steps with the excreta falling behind the pigs. This was so, for example, at three farms around Old Hutton, one of which an informant of mine used to have. The pigs were quite warm and comfortable, but when they were dispensed with (few pigs being kept locally), the part underneath was turned into a *duck-'ole*. The old word for such a toilet was the euphemism *necessary* (sometimes shortened to *netty* or *nessy*); and there is a story about one farmer who could not pay his rent and was solemnly warned by the agent to settle his arrears at once or else he would take the necessary steps. 'Thoo can tek the necessary an' the steps an' all,' said this farmer, ''cos there's plenty o' room behind t'edge.'

There is often humour in life's little tragedies. A very shy man had been engaged fifteen years but still did not like to be hurried. Public opinion summed up the acquaintance after the wedding: 'There's yan thing aboot it; it's nut so long to go if it don't turn out too well.' Two old Cumbrians met at the old Carlisle market, not having seen each other for several years. 'I'se nut forgitten thoo, Tom. I'se always watched t'papers to see if thoo's dead.' Boys too can be very mournful. A Westmorland farmlad was found sobbing beside a dead donkey. 'You must have been very fond of it?' queried a visitor. 'Nay, sir, I'se gitten t'job o' buryin' it.' Another anecdote tells of a young farmer, newly wed, who kept protesting to his wife about all sorts of household tasks, saying 'Mi mudder didn't do it that way.' Finally, when he voiced the same complaint about her churning, his exasperated wife simply pulled the bung out of the churn and let the cream run down the yeard, remarking, 'Did thi mudder ivver do that?' This year I noticed an Ambleside butcher and friend trying vainly to start a lady's car by pushing it downhill near Smithy Brow. 'Run it in t'beck if it won't go, then,' they finally told her.

A good many Cumbrian dialect jokes concern children; perhaps they, like the elderly, are in closer touch with dialect. Children's ideas are often so charmingly innocent. A Coniston teacher helped a boy to complete a painting by drawing fluffy white clouds. 'Where I come from, miss,' he argued, 't'clouds is mucky.' Farming interest was revealed in another Cumbrian lad who, when shown at Sunday school a picture of Jesus carrying a lamb, 'Does he leuk after hoggets as well?' Many of these stories prove Cumbrian *bairns* so steeped in local traditions and language that anything beyond is unknown and resented. A doctor recently moved from the South said to a sick girl, 'Open your mouth, child, and put out your tongue,' which met with nothing but a vacant stare. He then most tactlessly remarked to her mother, 'You must have a very stupid child, my good lady.' This brought, 'It's thoo at's stupid. Oppen thi gob, hinny, an' stick oot thi lolly.' Then the girl was all obedience, addressed in words she understood.

Now and then such stories, most of which are true, prove Cumbrian *bairns* quite brainy. Young Arthur ran to the *chimbley* calling, 'Fadder Christmas! Fadder Christmas! Ah wants a new bike.' Mother asked him to make less noise, adding, 'Father Christmas isn't deaf.' 'Ah knaws that,' said Arthur, 'but Granfadder is.' However, other tales show abysmal ignorance which even farm life has not yet corrected. Gordon, aged four, watched his father deliver a lamb. 'Hey, dad,' he asked, 'when did t'sheep eat t'lamb?' Mind you, parents must take their share of blame for their children's ignorance. This is indicated in many notes received by teachers, for example, 'Please excuse my son Fred being off school. He has had something the matter with his inside and it come out all over his face.

Another range of humorous anecdotes centres on Cumbria's sense of geography. There was the passenger on the British Rail vessel *Teal* who asked whether it stopped at Keswick; there was the child, told he was now back in Cumbria, saying, 'No, we're in t'car;' there was the woman who told her neighbour that her son was going to Hong Kong and, when asked which way, replied, 'Nay, I don't know, but he has to catch t'bus from Wukki'n. Confusion in distances is also a source of amusement—witness the claim that by car it is shorter from Bowness to Hawkshead than vice versa because of the way the roads bend; and that of the rural postman who said, 'Aye, it's a lang lonnin' (long lane) up to t'squire's, but if it was any shorter it wouldn't reach.'

Many laughable matters come to light simply because Cumbrians do not understand they are unintelligible. This generally happens through pronunciation and word choice. A railway porter, expected to shout, 'Aspatria. All change,' forgot the words and shouted, 'Speeatry. Loup out.' A Cockermouth teacher frowned at Marjorie. 'It's butter, dear - not botter,' she said patiently. Little Marjorie puzzled it out for a moment and then put up her hand. 'Please, miss, what do Ah say for jam?' At other times the root cause is misunderstanding of word meanings. 'Nice valley, this!' exclaimed a visitor from the States, 'Any celebrities been born round here?' 'Dunno what ye mean,' said the old inhabitant. 'Any big men been born here?', persisted the American, 'No, nowt but babies.' Still the tourist went on inquiring. 'Well, it feels healthy here. What's the death rate in this area?' 'Same as anywhere else,' he was answered, 'yaa death per person.' Yet occasionally this ignorance of word meanings seems to benefit the Cumbrian. 'I thought I told you to go on a diet,' said the doctor. 'Aye, yer did. Ah've had mi diet: this is mi dinner.'

Into this next section fit what we may call Cumbrian Irishisms, where the statement makes good sense to the speaker but not to listeners. For example: 'It's a ten-minute walk if thoo runs'; 'Anybody sittin' there?' (pointing to an empty seat); 'Is thoo readin' that paper thoo's sat on?; 'Is thoo in the till?' (postmistress to her assistant); 'There was neea gentlemen farmers, so we didn't talk to 'em.'

Some of the happenings in Cumbria sound quite astonishing. There is the busy manager at his Carlisle office-desk, already holding one phone and being presented with another by his clerk, who says, 'It's thoo.' There is the bleary-eyed drinker at a party who asks a beautiful lady, 'Can Ah walk thoo yam?' to be told abruptly, 'Yes, if you can remember where we live.' Some seem, in effect, a cry for help, as with the Lakeland *missus* who accompanied her husband for his medical check for life-insurance. She talked so much that the doctor, unable to get on with his job, pretended she was ill, popped a thermometer under her tongue and told her to hold it there for twenty minutes. As the couple left, the husband eagerly asked the doctor, 'Hoo much does yan o' them things cost?' All right, some of these yarns take a little believing, but the existence of varieties of humour up and down the county shows that Cumbrians do feel the need to laugh and are none the worse for it.

7. Occupational Dialect

It would be wrong to leave this Cumbrian book without considering words from different local occupations, for industrial language, besides having in its mix technical terms, abbreviations and slang, can also employ traditional local words.

First in fairness, even though it may seem outside the dialect pattern, we must mention Lakeland's great tourist industry. As the season approaches, in hotels and boarding-houses there is great dusting, mopping, painting, general polishing and *tittivating* and it seems *tittivating* of language too, for the industry yields few dialect treasures. You can hardly count cryptic notices like *b and b*, *dbb*, which in any case have become automatic visitors' language.

The tourist boom has not been good for dialects because tourists come from all over. Researchers tell us that 75 per cent of what is remembered comes through the sense of sight (which is what makes television so popular). Accordingly tourists love to see quaint things, but find it harder to understand quaint speech. They love to see Dove Cottage or Hornsea pottery, but may not notice a *yat* (gate) or *tll* (to) which is being said around them. It is urged that, just as Cumbrian farming and quarrying need to be preserved to prevent local occupations becoming entirely those represented in gift shops, so dialect has to be saved lest Cumbrian talk becomes over-refined and adapted to suit tourists. I wonder how far people will agree.

Potentially the most interesting language is that of farming, Britain's first occupation, simply because it is so deeply rooted in the past. Here survive many terms from what is often thought a bygone age, though Cumbria being a farming county has them in plenty. They have been treated in Chapter 4 and space forbids elaborating them here; but what should be noted is that farming terminology changes with the changing times. Just as *ploo-osses* and *flails* have given way respectively to tractors and modern methods of threshing, so the old-fashioned *shuppon* or *byre* is becoming the modern *cow-house* or *milkin'-parlour*.

Farmers co-operate with nature, but now we turn to two industries which disfigure the countryside, namely slate-quarrying and lead-mining. Many quarry words are old. One is *gavelock* for a crowbar, a word recorded in Lakeland in 1711. It was an important tool, for a quarryman's life could depend upon his *gavelock*. At Honister the *gant* was the platform fixed to a ladder-top. Blocks of slate called *clogs* were blasted from the rock. In former times these clogs were broken up by a great iron-bound mallet weighing over 30 lbs. and called *Big Mell.* The *rivers* in the slate quarries have a name going back to Scandinavian times (Old Norse *rífa*). They *rive,* literally 'tear', that is dress the blocks to single-slate thickness by hand, splitting them 'with the grain', after which the slate is called *rovven*. Best-quality slates are *fine metal* and second and third grades *grey metal,* somewhat confusing to the outsider who does not expect stone to be described as metal. Then for the final stages of production the *dressers* trim the rough edges of the slate to standard size. The slate is held over a fixed blade called a *brake* and a *whittle* (handknife) is brought down on the line of cut. So slate-quarrying is another industry rich in its special language.

For a long time lead-mining was important and Bavarian miners settled in Keswick in the second half of the sixteenth century. The richest vein in the Newland mountains was figuratively but very aptly called *Gowd(gold)Scalp*. The early pick and shovel gave way to gunpowder and then dynamite, quite disembowelling the mountain-sides. Fortunately the lead-mining was usually sporadic and the folds of the hills now hide what would in flat country be an unsightly mess. Blacklead is, curiously, not lead at all but almost entirely pure carbon. The 1541 rent rolls of Furness Abbey show that graphite, that is black lead, was then being mined opencast in Borrowdale. It was called *shepe oadde, black-cake* and *wadd,* and the substance was used for *smittlin'* sheep's fleeces with their farmer's brand-mark. Artists' pencils made with it used to be famous, as Keswick pencils still rightly are, but the blacklead is now imported.

Roadmaking used to be the domain of the *steean-napper,* who would sit at the roadside breaking up *steeans* (stones). They would arrive by *oss n' cart* to be tipped beside him, all as big as eggs. A passer-by could hardly tell that the *steean-napper* was a person, so shrouded was he under coats and sacks. You would just see the hands moving. He would sit for a week, piling up the stones round him in cubic yards, by which the parish council (for example, at Grasmere) paid him. There used to be no traffic danger with very few motor vehicles. The danger came from flying stones, to stop which he wore meshed spectacles.

Another old industry, and one which many Lakelanders would hate to see die, is that of building dry stone walls—*steean waws* or *dykes,* as they are called. They offer good shelter for sheep in a storm, being built on the cavity-wall principle, but often with *guts* (small stones) instead of proper cavities as in a house. At intervals there can be lines of *throughs,* reaching the whole width of the wall to stabilise it, no mortar or cement being used. The smooth respectable side of a stone wall is the *fyas(face)side,* and at corners are the *coin-ends*. The walls are well surmounted by *cams*, placed on a slant to let the water drain off. It is said that some of these Lakeland stone walls have stood for over two centuries, so durable are they against the wildest of storms. Old builders of stone walls are appalled to see the occasional house now erected of beautiful shaped stone. Facing-stone at today's prices costs a fortune, since it has to be cut into neat geometrical shapes, whereas formerly in house-building it did not matter.

The textile industry reached Cumbria. For example, around Grasmere there were *fullin -mills*, where cloth was thickened; and *Kendal bumpers* were local handloom weavers, so-called because of the sound they made as their feet stamped down on the pedals. Today's looms are quieter, but are still worked with the same terminology of *reeds, healds, and slays*. Notable in modern textiles is the *granny-shift* for married women while husbands look after the *kids*, for example at Ashley's in Ulverston or Lister's, the ring-spinners of Barrow.

Basket-making is a famous although almost extinct industry of South Cumbria. Basket-makers are known as *swillers*, which has nothing to do with the dictionary definition of a swiller as a drunkard. No-one seems to know why the oak *spale*(spell)-basket of Furness is called a *swill*, unless perhaps it is connected with *swirl* indicating the degree of roundness; for a swill is a cradle-shaped basket with an oval rim, called the *bool*, and a rounded bottom.

Such baskets have had various uses; for instance with gardeners for holding plants, weeds or light tools. Young mothers had a different use for them, for many a Furness child used to be rocked in a *swill*. *Swills* are made of hazel and oak, and the materials for them were plentiful because Furness used to be thickly wooded. The oak *spells* (ribs) and the *tahse* (lapping) are boiled twice. The oak is split with a *rivin'-knife* and then with a *settin'-in knife*, the process of *rivin'* (compare *rivin'* in slate-quarries above) meaning that the oak is literally torn into strips.

The *mare* is a treadle vice to hold the *spell* while it is being trimmed. The *swiller* sits at one end astride it: hence he rides the *mare*! Two other instruments of his are decidedly equestrian. His *set-horse* is a framework for shaping the *bool*; and his *split-horse* a lower framework to support the oak sapling whilst it is being split—hence its name. Naturally the special terms of this dying industry will not last for ever. The middle generation calls the ribs not *spell* but *laths*; and even people not averse to Cumbrian dialect, who refer, for example, to the *lugs* for the handles or 'big ears' of other baskets and to *cockan' a lug* for eavesdropping, call the traditional oak-*spell* baskets just *baskats*. As an industry dies, so does its terms.

The Solway is one of the very few places in England where *haaf-net* fishing is practised. It is a method of catching salmon and trout, though not very effective. *Haaf* comes from a Scandinavian word *haf* meaning 'sea', and it came to our country with the Norse settlers. The *haaf-net*, called round the River Lune the *lave-net*, is fixed to a sixteen feet long wooden frame divided by a vertical pole called a *haaf-balk*. The net, which resembles a huge shrimp-net, hangs from the frame in an enormous pouch. A *haaf-netter* wades into the Firth with *watter* swirling up to his *oxters* (armpits), holding the net against the flow of the tide.

Flookburgh, despite its apparently marine name, is so called not from Morecambe Bay *plaice-flukes* but from its founder *Flóki*. But it is renowned for cockling. Cockles are collected by a *craam*, a three-pronged fork, or else a *cockle-rake*. A wooden object, fascinatingly called from its size the *Jumbo*, agitates the sands to bring the cockles to the surface. It was invented over 90 years ago by Peter Butler of the well-known local fishing family. After they have been *craamed* or raked together, the cockles are put into sacks. In the hey-day of cockling, as many as ten wagon-loads of cockles were left at nearby Cark railway station in a day. Another device was the *push-net*, formerly used, for example, at Allonby for catching shrimps. The *pusher's* legs were wrapped with sacking to protect him against the *atterpile*, the small stinging-fish with three dorsal fins.

Knowledge of Cumbrian inshore-fishing expressions was greatly extended by the 1972 investigations of Willy Elmer, who visited Silloth, Maryport, Workington, Whitehaven, Haverigg, North Scale on Walney Island and Flookburgh. He uncovered many interesting terms, such as *snoodins* for a snood; and *cuvvin* (Maryport, Workington, Whitehaven), *whillock*, and *buckie* (Haverigg), all for a whelk. The fact that such terms change along a few miles of coast shows how isolated certain fishing villages must have been, and the danger of generalising about Cumbrian inshore-fishing language.

To consider in more detail terms from inshore fishing, along with coal-mining, steelmaking and building construction, I would refer readers to the Cumbrian section of my article in the 1968 Lancashire Dialect Society *Journal* on 'Fishing Language around England and Wales', and for all four industries in Cumbria to my analyses in The Lakeland Dialect Society *Journal* nos. 29 and 30. This seems a better plan than repeating everything here, with the added possibility of directing attention to other contents of those worthy journals. By this means we might even enrol some more outstanding members! However, to summarise here for those who prefer it: you might notice that coal-mining, an old industry, is chock-a-block with choice terms like *bink* for a mine-floor step and *cleat* for the grain in coal. Steelmaking too has plenty, though mixed with some flippancy and slang, as *chip-pan* or *kettle* for the electric-arc furnace; and building has a surprisingly varied array, including for instance Eskdale *jailin'* for wood's cracking and *witters* for the partitions between chimney flues.

To take another modern example, let us examine Kendal's

footwear industry. The parts of a boot include the *cap*, the *wing-vamp* across the instep, and the *quarter*. *Shanks* are steel supports for the underside of an arch, more often in ladies' shoes. *Shearlings* were offcuts and *feetage* was the maximum area of leather allowed for making so many pairs of shoes, a type of bonus being paid according to the *feetage*. The *clicker* cuts the uppers, the *clicking* process being followed by *skiving*, which does not mean shirking work in the slang sense but bevelling the edge. (Advertisements for *skivers* are quite common.) Then came *closing*, actually stitching the shoes, and *making* or finishing them. Incidentally, the well-known K for K-Shoes marked on the soles arose not for advertisement but to stop imitations. Here, then, is another industry contributing to the Cumbrian language-mix.

Obviously many industries have had to be omitted. Electrician's talk has not been discussed, for example, with its many abbreviations and slang terms like *juice* for current, nor the 'trade' language of bakers, nurses, and barbers (or, as they have nearly all quietly become, *gentlemen's hairdressers*). However, let us finish with a very modern industry, that of Barrow shipyards. Here you find that weird measurement a *shipwright's eighth*, comparable to a *baker's dozen*. Cumbrian welders suffer from what other dockyards call *arc-eyes*, for which the local word is *flash*. A welder will say, 'Ah've 'ad a flash,' to his doctor, who will write the term on a note. There is a good admixture of slang; so that some things are *shot at* (no good), and others never stolen but *swiped, nicked, pinched* or (rhyming slang) *'alf-inched*, etc. Types of rivets have their names, such as *flat-'eds* and *pan-'eds*. Parts of the shipyard include the *platers' sheds* and the *moul(d)-loft*, where ships' sections are marked out in wood high above ground because more space is available there.

The shipyard hierarchy embraces *t'gaffer* right down to the *'and-rag*, which stands for anyone at the bottom of the tree who is there to be *mucked about*. Among different occupations there are the *calkers* who calk rivets to ensure they are watertight: their name arose from such work on wooden boats but continues for similar work in metal. *Laggers* do the sound and heat insulating. Riveting includes a chain of sub-trades. The *chucker*, the man who with his tongs looks after the rivets in the fire, throws them up to the *catcher*, who catches them in a can. It is a continuous process to stop the rivets cooling. The *'odder-up* is a blacksmith's labourer who holds up the rivet as it is riveted. Without doubt, Cumbria's now standard language is not limited to general words: to hear it you must also follow the Cumbrian at work.

8. Local Glossaries

IN an enthralling article[1], R.S. Dilley of the University of Pittsburgh has noted that many traditional farming terms which are on dialect speakers' lips have appeared in manuscripts from 1500 onwards dealing with Cumberland lands. In the selection below from the article's list of ancient spellings, you will doubtless observe some for words that now seem extinct, others for live words mentioned elsewhere in this book, and others for words not yet instanced but living and known to you. Dialect has a long heritage.

bait: to feed, pasture
beald, bield: stone shelter, often in the form of a short wall, used on high and exposed fells to protect sheep from storms
beard: trim a hedge
bent: coarse grass
brig: build a bridge
cown, coom, comb: the dust and debris of peat
dike: hedge; wall
dubs: deep still pools in a river
eddish: aftermath
fleak, flake: hurdle, temporary fold or pen for sheep
gimmer: female yearling sheep
hogg: young sheep about a year old, before it has been shorn
lea: scythe
ling: heather
lonning, loaning: lane
march: boundary, landmark
neat: animal of the ox tribe, especially horned cattle (Still found in *neathouse:* cowhouse, cf. *Survey of English Dialects*)
rean, rane, rain, rayne: balk or strip of unploughed land
rigeld, ridgel: castrated horse
seaves: rushes
spelk: splinter
staddling: base of a stack
stang: pole, post or rail

1. Cumberland & Westmorland Antiquarian Soc. **Transactions**, new series, vol. LXX (1970), pp. 192-204.

stirk: young bullock or heifer, usually 1-2 years old
theak, thack: to thatch
toft: homestead
whin: gorse
wrack, wreck: seaweed

Ever since dialect investigation became a hobby, its devotees have rejoiced in gathering word lists. They appear in newspaper columns, exercise books etc., and soon no doubt we shall have them on tape. Among the best-known and most useful Cumbrian glossaries are the following:

Dickinson, W. *Glossary of the Words and Phrases of Cumberland,* 1859.
Ellwood, T. *A Glossary of Words in the Dialect of Cumberland, Westmorland and N. Lancashire,* 1895.
Kirkby, B. *Lakeland Words,* Wilson (Kendal), 1898.
Morris J.P., *Glossary of the Words and Phrases of Furness,* 1869.
Peacock R.B., *Glossary of the Dialect of the Hundred of Lonsdale,* 1869.
Relph, J.T., *Some Dialect Words 'Ta Deu Wid Sheep',* in Lakeland Dialect Society *Journal* no. 37 (a splendid list).

For the specialised vocabulary of fishing, in 1927 the Reverend S. Taylor provided a most accurate and detailed glossary of words then in use among the fishermen of Flookburgh[1], which every scholar of dialect in technical terms should consult. It included many words that suggest that the Flookburgh tradition goes back to Norse settlement, such as:

ask: cold, sharp (of wind)—NE Icel. *hask:* rough cold weather
hol: ditch, dyke—Old Norse (ON) *hol:* hole
melgreave: flow-hole, made in the sand by the tide—ON *melr* + *grof.*
mun: mouth—ON *munnr*
naff: nave of a wheel — ON *nof*
slatherly: dirty and drizzling, (of weather)—ON *sletta* bespatter
slemp: sly—ON (in the Edda) *sleyma:* a scamp
smoot in *gang smoot*: go home—ON *smuga:* hole
speel: wooden splinter—ON *spolr:* rail, spar
stang: cart-shaft—ON *stong*

Sad to say, after informal enquiry, Dr. Rollinson, of Liverpool University Extra Mural Department but himself a Barrow native stationed in Barrow, has found that only a few of those fishing words survive round Furness. The well-known glossaries were written last century and the ancient spelling evidence is from centuries earlier. We must therefore rely on modern conversations, dialect maps and other recent surveys, and I thus append in approximate

1. Cumberland & Westmorland Soc. **Transactions**, XXVII, pp. 152-163.

spelling dialect terms which reached my ears on recent visits to Cumbria but for which there is little space on other pages. I should be very grateful for any additions or qualifications that readers care to supply.

bag: cow's udder

bait: food taken to fields as dinner E.G. 'Where's mi bait-box?'

braffum, braffin: horse-collar

brew: make tea, (S. Cumbria). Otherwise *mask, mass* or *mash. Mak* is Cumbrian for 'make', but not of tea.

brig: bridge

brossen: inflated E.g. 'It's brossen', of an animal which has blown itself up by eating too much grass.

byre: old-fashioned cowhouse, (Penrith area as in adjacent Co. Durham). In Rydal etc. it is *shuppon*, with Northern *u* sound from Old English *y*. Parts of the *byre* include the *fodder-gang* (passage-way in front of cows), *boskin* (partition), *skellboos* (tethering-stake), *heelstone* (behind cow), *greeap* drain, and *round hank* (runner) on the *coo-band* (cow-tie).

caart: farm-cart. Its parts include *shafts, hay-shilvins* (extra side-pieces for carting hay), *heck* (back door), *hoop* (wheel hub) and *fellaz* (felloes, wooden sections of the rim).

cleg: horse-fly

coo-plat, coo-clap, cow-swat: clot of cow dung

coppy: stool. *Coppies* (three-legged milking-stools) were invariably used, for example around Rydal since they were steadier *on t'shuppon flooar*.

flay-crow: scarecrow

geeas: goose

gripe: three-pronged garden fork

hoggast: small shed for *beasts*, animals. There are several, for example, on the way from Eden Hall to *Gert Saffel* (Great Salkeld)

jannock: fair E.g. It's nut jannock.

kaff: chaff

lap: to wrap

ley: scythe (still a very common word).

lile: little

mawnt: mustn't

mistetched, of a *hoss* pulling,: suddenly finding it too much and slipping backwards.

moo and *myoostead*: hay-bay. A *sunken moo* is below ground level in the barn, to keep the hay very dry to prevent spontaneous combustion.

muck-midden: manure heap, formerly made of *streea* (straw) and *muck*.

nayder: neither

neean, neen, nin: none

nowt (rhyming with Standard English *out*): nothing

pap and (politer) *quaarter*: teat. E.G. 'She's deeaf (deaf) i' yaa pap,' or, 'She's leet (light) of a quaarter,' of a cow not producing milk from one teat. 'There's nowt like a pap for 'im to sowk (suck) at, even if it's a deaf 'un,' of a young bull-calf being reared for service.

ploo: plough. Its parts include *ploo suck* (plough sock), *mowd-booard* (mouldboard) and *cooter* (coulter).

Queer Feller: Old Barrow word for a freemason, so-called because they went to lunch on Wednesday carrying their little cases.

racks: cart-ruts

recklin (usual), *weedlin, winklin:* smallest and weakest pig of a litter

reeans: reins

savvins: juniper trees on the fell side, growing only six to twelve feet high E.g. 'Wheer's t'hounds gone?'. 'Into yon savvins.

scrow: mess, a term used on Kendal-area farms every day. E.g. 'This is an awful scrow.'

shive: slice of bread

skirl, shirl, slur: to slide

smiddy: smithy

stee: ladder

stiles of many types, including *squeezer stiles* with V-shaped openings; and *kissin'-yats* (kissing-gates), named not from lovers' kisses but less romantically because the *yat* kisses or touches the two *stoops* (posts) between which it swings. The *hingins* are the hinges.

switch, slash, splash, snaze, dress: trim (a hedge)

thrang: busy E.g. 'What's thoo thrang wid today?'

towp: tip up E.g. 'Yer caart's gaan to towp.'

trunlins: sheep or rabbit droppings

yan, yaa: one E.g. 'Yan of his', 'Thoo'll be gittin' wed yaa day.'

9. Now and the Future

TO assess the future of Cumbrian dialects, we must first remind ourselves of their general picture today, which is of a group of very different members. The rural dialects are easily the richest in traditional words, followed by the old West Cumbrian mining areas and fishing localities like Flookburgh. To sample the current mixture, let us highlight the speech of certain areas, taking them for ease of reference alphabetically.

BARROW has been subjected to many outside influences, with settlers from Belfast and Glasgow and much immigration in war-time, when the town was so geared to the armaments drive. Barrow has affinities with industrial areas of Lancashire—indeed, listening to chance conversations in its streets, you can be forgiven for thinking that you are in a Lancashire town. There are frequent glottal stops as in "Ave yer go' i' (got it)?', a very diphthongised 'long oo' sound in for example 'We tOOk a lOOk at the bOOk', and undiphthongised *aw* in *naw* (no), *gaw* (go) etc., although more educated Barrovians have eradicated these elements from their speech. It is perhaps the urban-rural split which makes Barrow link more with Lancashire towns and Ulverston instead of with rural Lakeland. Barrovians are apt to be insular, out on a limb. Their be-all-and-end-all is said to be to sit out on Walney Island (which, by the way, my wife did not recognise until someone told her she was on it), and allegedly their idea of a good day out is indulging in bingo at Blackpool. These claims are certainly exaggerated, but Barrow with its dialect, though now set within the Cumbrian framework, is quite individualistic.

CARLISLE, as Chapter 5 shows, has a dialect as different as the proverbial chalk from cheese. It has a marked Northern flavour, in a few words like *cuddy* a strong North-Eastern connection, and to most residents of Southern Cumbria has a definite Scottish lilt.

CARTMEL has had the dual function of nurturing fishermen-farmers, so producing a dialect with a strangely varied technical element, strong in Icelandic words. A Cartmel man billeted in Iceland in 1940-1 when Britain occupied that territory for a year before the Americans took over, made himself understood by using his dialect words such as *balk* for a type of net (Old Norse *balkr*).

Since the KENDAL area is thoroughly immersed in farming

dialect, it is a source for ancient terms. *Coo-bands* (cow-ties), *leys* (scythes) and all the rest are just technical terms round here, so you must not be too put out by rough-sounding instructions like, 'Keck (tip) t'arse-end o' t' cart'. Even *boon days* (on April 5th, when tenant farmers changed their farms) are remembered.

MILLOM, like Askam farther south, is a very friendly close-knit community. Influxes of labourers, many Irish, to the steelworks have done little to its language. It has no glottal stop; though it does have other ties with north Lancashire in its undiphthongised *ay*, in for instance, *trade* and *aw* in words like 'know' instead of 'the Queen's *oh.*' For example Millom schoolchildren say, 'Dawn't Whitehaven people speak awful!', whereas they find the talk of young friends from Barrow quite ordinary. This fits, because the Duddon estuary is really only a continuation of Morecambe Bay.

The PENRITH area, like that of Kendal, has a strong agricultural bias and so relies greatly on traditional language. For remarks like 'Ista gaily gaan aboot?' (i.e. Are you well?) and 'What (rhyming with *cat*)'s ta gaan ta deea (do) toneet?' a Penrith man and his pal were mistaken in the R.A.F. as having come from the Hebrides. The district is also charged with being notable for bulky farmers with peculiar, whining, high-pitched voices (Co. Durham type, not Welsh). At all events, it has about the most extreme variety of Cumbrian.

WINDERMERE by contrast is thought a most 'civilised' village; but even here it depends on who is being heard, and it is not difficult to bob into various households there and immediately find oneself in a world of 'oot o' t' rooad' (out of the way), *nowt* (nothing) and 'Thoo waint finnd (won't find) it'.

As for WORKINGTON and WHITEHAVEN, their mining background helps to give a historical air to their local speech, which has certain words like *marrer* (mate) akin to those of the North-East. Their type of dialect appears to be spreading to factory girls in Cockermouth and even Keswick.

Thus, having tried to summarise the present 'state of play' in Cumbrian dialects, we turn to the future. The first thing to observe is that, whatever dialect traces you retain after your formative years, say up to the age of twenty, are likely to remain. Broad-speaking Cornish tin-miners who were above that age when they reached Millom kept their 'Where be 'ee to?' type of South-Western dialect to their dying day. Similarly any broad-spoken Cumbrian adult is not going to have his speech significantly altered by a package holiday to Majorca or by visits to his children in Canada. The son of a Windermere native left there at sixteen, but when aged forty nine was recognised abroad by a stranger on the phone as having come from Windermere. Similar cases are not unknown, for dialect, when it is well embedded in youth, will last.

The point is repeatedly made that television, radio, mass

education and ease of travel have subjected dialects to an increasing battering of 'acceptable' language. This is undeniable and yet, perversely it seems, dialect has suddenly gained respect, thanks chiefly to regional broadcasting. Formerly, if an interviewer brought out a tape-recorder, he would be asked suspiciously, 'What's ta gitten theer?'; now I am sometimes asked why I have not brought one. Yet in other ways conditions today are harder. Previously, chances of hearing wonderful dialect were so many that they went unnoticed. At the time, we do not realise the strangeness of what we hear as a child. As a helper ruefully told me about the words and yarns he met as a lad. 'We should 'ave wrote 'em'.

I must issue two gentle warnings, however. Dialect enthusiasts would not like this revival of interest to be in reverse proportion to its usefulness, like the growing keenness to acquire grandfather clocks, old chimney pots and cartwheels which now have little use except for ornament. Nor must we, in eagerness to study dialect, exaggerate what survives. I have heard it said that Wastdale Head had 't' deepest lake, t' heeast fell and t' biggest leear—he lived at t' pub'. Not only is the first claim subject to attack by lovers of Ullswater, who argue that in that lake could be put the surrounding mountains upside down, and the third claim rather exaggerated in its reference to Eric Ritson, but *heeast* and *leear* are no longer standard Cumbrian. The well-known claim was repeated in more normal dialect on a 1978 television programme. On the lake-depths and Eric Ritson's morals someone else must pontificate; but for dialect a middle course is here recommended, between trying to resurrect what is extinct and arguing that no true dialect is left.

What of the future? Dialect is not dying out in Barrow, Whitehaven, Workington or even the 'capital', Carlisle. It is mixing but not changing entirely—for example, Barrovians are not going to talk a variety of Scouse. Dialect is spreading, as ever, along main lines of communication: consequently big estates constructed round Ulverston, for instance, now rear a town-type dialect, and the pattern is repeated on the fringes of other Cumbrian urban areas.

People seem to think the dialects of industrial areas bad, rough or uncouth. They grumble, for example, that Millom speech is being diluted. But what speech are they diluting? Its population was probably only about fifty rural workers before the erection of the steelworks, and so its more representative dialect is its later one. Do let us keep things in proportion.

It is notable—some say heartening—that many Cumbrian youngsters, for example at Penrith comprehensive schools, still speak dialect, which suggests that historical dialect in Cumbria has still a significant future. Furthermore the county has some daleheads and isolated villages which are still so remote that they are likely to retain their dialect much longer than has been the case in other English shires where such talk is rapidly being engulfed in that of nearby larger villages and towns. Also, although Cumbria's industrial language will alter as new processes and industries appear whilst others fade, Britain as an industrial nation will never allow its industry and the accompanying varieties of language to die.

It seems certain, therefore, that despite changes Cumbria's independent forms of speech will live on for the benefit of scholars, visitors and—far more important—Cumbrians themselves, reminding them of so much that is sensible and worth preserving in their cultural heritage.

For Further Reading

Brilioth, B., *Grammar of the Dialect of Lorton (Cumberland)*, Oxford, 1913.

Brook, G.L., *English Dialects*, Deutsch, 1963; and *Varieties of English*, Macmillan, 1973.

Denwood, E.R. and M., *Oor Mak o' Toak: an anthology of Lakeland Dialect Poems 1747-1946*, Lakeland Dialect Soc., 1946.

Ekwall, E., *Oxford Dictionary of English Place-Names*, O.U.P., 3rd ed., 1947.

Ellis, A.J., *Early English Pronunciation, Part V*, E.E.T.S., 1889; and *English Dialects—their Sounds and Homes*, E.E.T.S., 1890.

Ellwood, T. (ed.), *Anderson's Cumberland Ballads and Songs*, Holmes (Ulverston), 1904.

Gibson, A.C., *Folk Speech of Cumberland and some Districts Adjacent...*, Coward (Carlisle) and J.R. Smith (London), 1869.

Hirst, T.O., *Grammar of the Dialect of Kendal (Westmorland)*, Heidelberg, 1906.

Kirkby, B., *Lakeland Words*, Wilson (Kendal), 1898.

Kolb, E., *Phonological Atlas of the Northern Region*, Francke Verlag, Bern, 1966.

Lakeland Dialect Society, *Journal*, 1939 Onwards. Full sets of copies in the public libraries of Barrow, Carlisle and Lancaster.

Nicholson, N., *The Lake District: an Anthology*, Robert Hale, 1977.

Orton, H. et al., *Survey of English Dialects*, Arnold (Leeds), 1962-71.

Orton, H. and Wright, N., *Word Geography of England*, Seminar Press, 1974.

Partridge, E., *Dictionary of Slang and Unconventional English*, 1961.

Reaney, P.H., *Grammar of the Dialect of Penrith*, Manchester University Press, 1927.

Skeat, W.W., *English Dialects from the Eighth Century to the Present Day*, Cambridge, 1911.

Wakelin, M.F. (ed.), *Patterns in the Folk Speech of the British Isles* and (author) *English Dialects: an Introduction,* Athlone Press, 1972.

Wright, J., *English Dialect Dictionary,* 6 vols., Oxford, 1898-1905.

Wright P., *Language of British Industry,* Macmillan, 1974.

Index